The Power of
MAGNETIC
LEADERSHIP

It's Time to Get R.E.A.L.

BY DIANNE DURKIN WITH CAREY EARLE

In memory of my father, Joseph S. Michonski,
my rock and my inspiration, who passed on December 28, 2010

ForeWord Reviews

ForeWord Clarion Reviews
BUSINESS & ECONOMICS
July 1, 2011

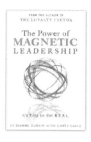

The Power of Magnetic Leadership:
It's Time to Get R.E.A.L.
Dianne Durkin with Carey Earle
CreateSpace
978-1-4537-5123-7
Five Stars (out of Five)

Getting "R.E.A.L." as a leader, according to author Dianne Durkin, results in an inviting workplace with engaged employees. This philosophy is what Durkin offers in her slim volume geared toward middle and upper-level managers. Her twenty-five years of experience as a consultant, trainer, motivational speaker, and author lend creditability to The Power of Magnetic Leadership. She conveys serious workplace issues in a breezy, conversational style often used in management seminars.

This is a to-do book. Filled with self-assessment tools to help determine personal management style, listening skills, and life goals, it prompts the reader to reflect on many of the most critical issues facing today's managers. Her acronym, R.E.A.L., is the focus of the book: Recruiting, Engaging, Appreciating, and Leading. Sprinkled throughout the book are R.E.A.L. tips intended as quick lessons.

Durkin uses examples from a number of well-known businesses, including JetBlue, Swedwood (IKEA), Sony Pictures, Nike, and Starbucks, to drive home the importance of vision and value statements and employee recognition programs. She presents realistic work-life situations in covering interview strategies, listening skills, and coaching techniques. Durkin offers a number of ideas for employee recognition and appreciation depending on an organization's budget. Simple work environment enhancement ideas are presented. Her section on generational differences is particularly valuable; what motivates baby boomers won't necessarily inspire the millennial generation. She also provides a list of characteristics of magnetic leaders along with several examples of quality leadership and emphasizes the importance of health and fitness to avoid physical and mental burnout. In addition, Durkin offers tips on how to effectively use technology as a manager in today's wired, global economy.

The author places a great deal of emphasis on communication, especially when speaking with employees. Without clear, direct communication, asking critical questions, and listening carefully, she argues, it is difficult to build trust and loyalty with employees and customers. To make her point, she employs a number of examples and exercises to develop effective listening skills.

Graphics enhance the text and help the reader better understand concepts and statistical reports. She frequently cites studies and news reports in support of her management lessons. The book is well organized, building on each chapter.

Magnetic leadership is possible for most anyone committed to creating a better work environment. Durkin's book is a great pep talk and valuable asset for those with the vision and commitment to be good leaders.

Mary Cary Crawford

Table of Contents

Acknowledgments

I would especially like to thank Cristina Barnard who besides being the most amazingly positive person in the world, it is my good fortune to have her as my operations manager. No matter what life challenges come her way, she remains positive, upbeat and energized to handle the situation to perfection. She is an inspiration to me and everyone she comes in contact with.

Cristina, thank you so much for being you, keeping me on track and having an uncompromising dedication and commitment to Loyalty Factor.

Dianne M. Durkin

Introduction

What is Magnetic Leadership? The answer to that question comes from defining what it is not. Uninspired leadership that disengages employees is the "reverse polarity" of Magnetic Leadership.

Think of the successful professional who may have climbed the ladder without ever learning how to play well with others.

Think of leadership that does not connect with people because the vision and purpose are not relevant to them.

Think of leadership that talks without listening.

Think of leadership that promises without delivering.

Think about the cost of unengaged employees.

According to pollster Gallup, actively disengaged employees cost the U.S. workforce more than $300 billion in lost productivity alone. How much is employee disengagement costing you?

If you have weak or non-existent leadership in your organization, it is like spraying a big can of people repellent into the air that your employees breathe. You kill creativity, productivity and the spark that ignites new ideas. You risk losing top talent and cultivating people with promise

Here is the good news: you can create Magnetic Leadership in your organization. And you do not have to look like a rock star or a celebrity to do it. You just have to have heart, be open to some organizational soul searching, and most importantly, you have to be real. Take an active interest in others. Listen to people and act decisively and consistently based on what you hear.

In this book, I will show you how to transform your organization, energize your employees and boost your bottom line with The Power of Magnetic Leadership. I will use the R.E.A.L acronym as our guideposts, revealing the meaning throughout this book. You will look at yourself as a leader and ask some hard questions along the way. Each answer brings you closer to being a Magnetic Leader who inspires others in your organization.

Are you ready?

Let's get R.E.A.L.

Chapter One
Cultures to Create Measureable Results

> *"The true essence of leadership is that you have to have a vision. You can't just blow an uncertain trumpet."*
>
> —*Theodore Hesburgh*

There are many myths about leadership that often prevent people from developing their leadership skills. They think if they were not born a leader with some magic leadership dust in their DNA, they cannot become one in the future.

While some people may be more natural leaders than others, some of the best leaders I have worked with are men and women who went beyond cultivating their own leadership skills and instead created a culture of leadership in their organizations. In this book, that is what I am going to bring to life for you – the reality that leadership does not belong to just one person. Leadership inspires others and becomes a contagious force. In this chapter, I explore vision, purpose, values, trust and how they are all part of your role as a leader. In chapter two, there are some tools to help you evaluate yourself as a leader and accountability tools to keep you on track.

Great Leaders Realize that Leadership Is an Engine

It is an engine of innovation that runs on change, truth, communication and vision. Great leaders make a difference in the lives of their people, their organizations and the processes. In chapter three, I look at how to recruit and retain the best people. With the right people on board, there is nothing an organization cannot accomplish.

Great leaders encourage their people to bring their brains to work.

The fastest way to lower the IQ of an organization is to create a culture where people only follow the rules and never think outside their job descriptions. In chapter four, I explore how to fully engage and empower your employees, so they are always thinking and contributing their best.

Great Leaders Appreciate People and Let Them Know It

Again and again, I have seen this in my work with organizations. Money is not the motivator. What people want is for work to fulfill a basic emotional human need; they want to feel appreciated. In chapter five, I focus on appreciation and the importance of rewarding and recognizing people.

Great Leaders Create Loyalty

Leadership is not an ego game. It is purpose driven. I heard Frances Hesselbein, president and CEO of the Leader to Leader Institute and former CEO of Girl Scouts of America, speak at a conference where she addressed the Women President's Organization. In her presentation, she told the audience that great leaders always put purpose first—never their own egos. In chapter six, I look at traits of outstanding leaders, two case studies that show Magnetic Leadership in motion and how the health of the CEO can be a model for the health of an organization.

Great Leaders Look Ahead

In chapter seven, I look at the future of leadership. From the power of social media and technology to the importance of a global perspective, we see how Magnetic Leadership will be even more important in an age of increased transparency.

Great Leaders Take Action

In chapter eight, you can start your engines. We end with 10 steps you can immediately implement.

I know it sounds like a lot to tackle. It is really about going back to basics. In each chapter, I will talk about how you can get R.E.A.L. about becoming a Magnetic Leader:

Here is how this book is going to help you get R.E.A.L.

Recruitment that gets the right people on the bus in the right spots and also shows you how to Retain them.

Engaging, Empowering and Enriching employees and providing the right Environment for success. I will take you through the Big E and show you why this vowel rocks an organization in the most powerful of ways.

Appreciating people. What do people want most? It is not money. It is to be valued, rewarded and recognized.

Leadership that leads to loyalty. Leadership is not about ego. It is the opposite. It is about purpose first. When leadership attracts the right people, engages, empowers and appreciates them, the result is loyal, productive employees.

So, are you ready to get started? Let us kick it off with a powerful trio.

Vision. Purpose. Values: A Powerful Trio

So, where do you begin this leadership journey? Before you can rally the troops, you have to have a compelling vision. Now, do not sigh. I know what you are thinking. You have been through a million visioning exercises.

Vision gets a bad rap in many organizations because too many people have sat through a PowerPoint™ presentation where management presents a vision, and then it promptly disappears forever. And what happens? People feel cheated. They feel like an outsider, not the insider they want to be.

It does not have to be that way. When vision comes to life in an organization, it is powerful, and it changes the status quo forever.

People want to see change that is meaningful. They want you to tell them the truth, communicate regularly, and they want a vision they can believe in and follow. For that to happen, you need vision and its two dance partners: purpose and values.

Moving Mountains

When you couple vision with purpose and values, everyone is dancing together. It is an unbeatable trio that can move mountains.

1.   Vision expresses where you are going.

Vision is what brings your employees to the dance floor. It is a clear picture of the future that inspires people.

I want to caution you to avoid the natural temptation to write one of those long, rambling paragraphs that includes all the buzzwords du jour. That is not a vision. It is a long paragraph no one will remember. Instead, state your future in a clear, concise statement that motivates and engages.

2.   Purpose is simple.

Purpose answers two questions: What business are you in, and what difference are you making in this world?

3.   Clear values.

What guides your behavior and the decisions you make on a daily basis? This is the "how" part of your vision. While you may not write it in the statement, it is how the statement comes alive because this is how you behave every day. You need to communicate these values, and then lead by example as you demonstrate these values in your decisions and actions.

Examples of Inspiring Vision Statements

Yes, anyone can write a run-of-the-mill vision statement. Do not do that. Remember that your vision needs to create a picture your organization can see and understand. So make sure your vision paints that kind of picture. The picture can, of course, connect to business goals and spreadsheets. That is for the meeting with the chief financial officer. To inspire and unite your organization, you want simplicity, clarity and a spark that ignites the imagination—not a rambling paragraph.

Here are three that inspire me.

If you have a body, you are an Athlete.

This was an original vision statement of Nike, coined by Nike co-founder Bill Bowerman[ii]. The picture it paints is clear – everyone has the potential to be an athlete, and so everyone is a potential customer of Nike. This statement has a more emotive purpose because it goes beyond "we sell sneakers" to "we sell inspiration." This is in the same spirit as Just Do It, their memorable and often-quoted tagline.

We bring humanity to the air.

This was a vision statement shared in a JetBlue letter to shareholders several years ago, and it still remains firmly entrenched in my mind. It is one of the best vision statements I have ever read. I love the purpose of this one because it reminds employees they are not just flying people from point A to point B. They are in the business of providing people with a good experience in the air. The statement is a challenge to change the way people view air travel. The picture of the future that it conjures is one of happy, smiling passengers versus what many think of when boarding an airplane.

To inspire and nurture the human spirit—
one person, one cup and one neighborhood at a time.[iii]

This is from Starbucks, and it is on their web site as their mission. However, I see it as a great vision statement because it is not talking about how much coffee the company is going to sell. It talks about the picture that is painted when employees do their job right. Starbucks has known for a long time that the company is not selling coffee. It is selling an experience. It is a haven in the middle of a busy day. Starbucks wants to inspire and nurture us. Guess where this vision needs to resonate? With the people making your grande latte. That is a challenge we all can relate to. No matter the size of your business, you have to infuse that vision throughout your organization.

Committing to World Class Growth with World Class People
Building Simple Elegance
Living the Swedwood Way of life

This is the three-part vision of Swedwood America, the first manufacturing plant in the United States that builds furniture for IKEA®. It contains the purpose (Building Simple Elegance), the vision for the future (Committing to World Class Growth with World Class People) and how to achieve the purpose and vision. Swedwood expands the value statements to communicate to employees what their role is in this vision.

What is World Class?

At Swedwood America, it means performing at a level above average, giving 100 percent year after year and performing beyond all international organizations everywhere. It is exceeding customer expectations and hiring world class people.

Building Simple Elegance

This is the company's distinction in the marketplace—to provide affordable and simple elegance to people all over the world.

Living the Swedwood Way of Life

The golden rule within the organization is to be the best you can be, and work as a team to help others be the best they can be. This translates into operating with integrity, honesty and respect; striving for excellence, safety and quality; and communicating as a team. Their values are clear, and the expectations are set and tied to the performance appraisal process. Everyone knows how to live the Swedwood Way of Life.

Swedwood Way of Life

Respect
"Treat Others the Way You Want to be Treated"

Integrity
"Doing the Right Thing"

Safety
"Safety First"

Quality
"Customer Satisfaction"

Teamwork
"Together Everyone Achieves More"

Communication
"Everyone Needs to Know"

Values in Motion

If you think about how you want people to behave (treat each other and treat clients, vendors and partners) this will guide you to create your values.

Below are some values that people can identify with:

Collaboration	Enthusiasm
Creativity	Friendliness
Accountability	Imagination
Agility	Service
Compassion	Trust

Here are the values of the Coca-Cola Corporation as expressed on their web site[iv]:

Our values serve as a compass for our actions and describe how we behave in the world.

Leadership
The courage to shape a better future.

Collaboration
Leverage collective genius.

Integrity
Be real.

Accountability
If it is to be, it is up to me.

Passion
Committed in heart and mind.

Diversity
As inclusive as our brands.

Quality
What we do, we do well.

JetBlue Airways has both values and five principles of leadership[v]

Values	Five Principles of Leadership
Safety	Inspire greatness in everyone.
Caring	Treat people right.
Integrity	Do the right thing.
Fun	Communicate with your team consistently.
Passion	Encourage initiative and innovation.

Whole Foods describes their values as the soul of their company[vi].

- Selling the highest quality natural and organic products available.

- Satisfying and delighting our customers.

- Supporting team member happiness and excellence.

- Creating wealth through profits and growth.

- Caring about our communities and our environment.

- Creating ongoing win-win partnerships with our suppliers.

- Promoting the health of our stakeholders by educating them about healthy eating.

A R.E.A.L. Tip

If you met one of your employees on the street, would she know what your company's values are? Think about ways to communicate **and** activate them!

Participation Is a Two-Way Street

A living and thriving vision sounds like a tall order if you think you can create it in one meeting. Show a video, write a new vision statement and everyone feels good, right? Wrong! You need to embrace a living, thriving vision as an organizational priority and a job where everyone is on the dance floor. It is not a lofty concept reserved for the corporate elite and world leaders. It becomes an irresistible force when it is participatory—not passive. Participation means everyone is involved.

Consider a former New York-based HMO that served 95,000 members. In August 2003, the CEO unexpectedly passed away, and the former executive director assumed the CEO responsibilities. With a grieving staff and the company at a critical juncture, she was only weeks away from the annual retreat. She seized the opportunity and decided to create the company's first formal mission statement at the retreat. She divided all four hundred employees into twenty teams and announced that their goal was to have a fully crafted mission statement by the close of the session on the next business day. She asked each team to answer five questions:

1. **As a company, what is it that we believe?**
2. **What are we in business to do, and what do we do exceedingly well?**
3. **What is unique about the way we do it?**
4. **What makes us innovative?**
5. **What makes us a great place to work?**

The new CEO and her team assembled all the teams' notes that night and developed a draft of the mission statement. She told the group it took about an hour because there had been so much alignment in the messages.

When she read the mission statement aloud, there was a sense of pride in the room. People could hear their words and phrases reflected in the statement.

The HMO's mission statement

We provide health insurance, preventive care education and compassionate care to those with important health-care needs. We do this by going the extra mile to develop trusting relationships with our diverse communities. We strive to reach every family we can serve. We are dedicated to making dreams come true—one child, one family, one community at a time.

Dianne M. Durkin with Carey Earle

The CEO modeled the importance of participation as a two-way street. She did not just give a pep-rally speech. Instead, she engaged her employees in crafting a mission and being part of creating the future. When participation starts with each individual—and with leaders living the vision, the values and purpose of the organization—you have the foundation of trust.

Trust is the foundation and framework of all relationships

There was a reason that your mother and father stressed the importance of telling the truth. They wanted you to understand the social implications of trust. When people do not trust you, they do not want to play with you. This was not only true in grade school; it is especially true in organizations of every size, shape and culture.

I remember once in a meeting a man said to me:

"Trust is a 'nice to have,' but let's face it,
you don't need it to get work done."

And I asked him this question:

"Do people communicate openly and honestly without trust?"

He thought for a moment and then said:

"Probably not."

"And, why would you say that most mistakes
happen in an organization?"

"Communication breakdown." he answered rather sheepishly.

Think of disasters that happen in every industry. Many of them go back to a communication breakdown, and if you dig even further, you find a lack of trust that prevented people from speaking up or raising a red flag.

Establishing Trust

What you say and what you do need to match. If they are incongruent, then your word is meaningless. It is all about communicating with honesty and straightforwardness. When we communicate effectively, people feel safe, comfortable and understood. It is important to communicate and share all information you have, and tell people what you know even when there is nothing to report or when there is negative information. People want honest information so they can make appropriate decisions that work for them based on that information. When there is silence in your organization, the grapevine takes over.

Reality Check with #1

Trust begins within each and every one of us. Here are five key questions to ask yourself:

1. **Are you honest with yourself about who you are and how you live your life?**
2. **Is your character solid?**
3. **Does 'yes' really mean 'yes' and 'no' really mean 'no'?**
4. **Do you follow through on your commitments?**
5. **Do you own up to your mistakes?**

Trust Builders

Once you have looked at yourself, you need to look at your team and develop behaviors that build trust throughout the organization. Congruence, reliability, acceptance and openness are our four trust builders that can transform an organization when applied consistently.[vii]

Trust Builders

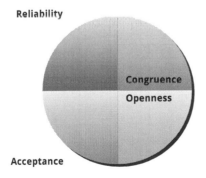

Under each of our trust builders, there are two values that drive the overall behavior. These are the "hows." For example, how do you get congruence? You are straightforward and honest.

Congruence means people consistently seeing that what you say is true.

Straightforwardness

- Provides clear expectations.

- Discusses and resolves disagreements with no animosity brewing beneath the surface.

- Discusses and recognizes individual performance and improvement. There are no grey, murky areas that are unclear.

Honesty

- Demonstrates high standards of honesty in everything you do.

- Does not tolerate hidden agendas or political power plays.

Openness means you have an environment where people are comfortable participating and contributing.

Receptivity

- Gives new ideas and methods a fair hearing.

- Encourages innovation and creativity.

- Allows individuals to take risks.

Disclosure

- Encourages open communication of ideas and opinions.

- Ensures frequent, clear, consistent and concise exchange of information.

Acceptance says: "I'm okay. You're okay." Differences are welcome.

Respect

- Values people for who they are and accepts differences from culture to style to ethnicity.

- Respects people for their contributions.

- Maximizes people's strengths and develops areas for improvement.

Recognition

- Recognizes good work and rewards results.

- Recognizes people fairly and consistently.

Reliability creates an organization of go-to people.

Excellence

- Individuals seek excellence in everything they do.

- People perform beyond expectations.

Commitments

- People follow through on their commitments and responsibilities.

- People can count on one another and their management for support.

Of course, these are all just words until people see them in action. You can write down that respect, honesty, straightforwardness and keeping commitments are core values. The magic happens when you explain how people can experience these in their workplace. Let us look at how WOW statements can do that for you.

A R.E.A.L. Tip

Think of trust as a bank account. If you keep making deposits, it will grow. Each time you do something negative, you spend money. Do enough negatives due to lack of character or competence, and you are bankrupt, and that is the end of the relationship.

The Wallop of a "WOW"

WOW statements are a simple and effective way to build a culture based on the core values of an organization and to bring these core values to life. They go a long way toward creating respect, trust and loyalty.

The premise of a WOW statement is that every interaction communicates value and is an opportunity to WOW someone. Here are some examples of WOW statements in action:

An employee goes above and beyond to solve a customer-service issue. You recognize her by saying: "Jody, you really represented us well today by making the customer feel like the most important person in the world. When you do this, you help us build our business through outstanding customer service."

You are a manager on a manufacturing line. There is a technology issue, and the line has been down. You jump in to help and get operations back quickly. One of your team members says: "Thanks for jumping in there." And you respond with: "We are all on a team here, and whatever I can do to support you and our team, I will do." WOW. That is a great manager, reinforcing the team culture.

You are managing a project team, and people have been pushing very hard to make a deadline. You tell your team you appreciate everything they are doing. One of your employees responds: "You have not seen anything yet!" That is a WOW statement. The values of hard work and a sense of accomplishment are being truly lived by the employees.

You are a manager of customer-service representatives at an airline ticket counter. The passengers are frustrated because of delayed flights. One of your fellow customer-service representatives is dealing with an angry customer. You walk over and say: "Let me help out here for a minute. I know it is easy for everyone to get frustrated over flight delays. Tell me about your situation." You diffuse the situation by WOWing the customer into explaining the problem before things heat up further. You WOW your teammate by letting her take a step back, and you employed empathetic listening, which I will take a closer look at in chapter three.

What makes WOW statements work? They have to be authentic and both substantiate and emphasize values you are trying to build in the organization – good customer service, teamwork, respect for others, work ethics, etc.

Take a moment to think of a recent situation where you could have used a WOW statement.

Write a few WOW statements that you, as a leader, can use with the people in your organization. A WOW statement recognizes when someone is living the core values of the organization and helps them understand the importance of those core values to drive success. Remember, these WOW statements need to be sincere and have passion and energy.

Your own WOW Statements

_____

_____

_____

_____

_____

Feels good to write them, right? Feels even better to say them. Put some WOW statements to work for you today!

You can begin to see how Purpose, Vision and Values work together in an organization. WOW statements help to express the vision and values and bring them to life. Magnetic Leadership is not a "top down" management style. Instead, it is inclusive, inviting and welcomes all employees to participate.

Once you have the powerful trio clearly and concisely defined and communicated, empower each department to set specific goals and processes to achieve the vision and values. Make sure you clearly outline individual roles and responsibilities, explain departmental and individual goals and align them with the overall vision of the organization.

Communication cannot be underestimated. In this process, you cannot over communicate. When the leaders clearly define their purpose, vision and values, and build an organization based on trust, it establishes a culture of responsibility across the organization.

The Purpose Pyramid below gives you a top-line view of how your Magnetic Leadership will spread throughout your organization and to all departments.

Purpose: why we exist...achieving the reason the organization was created, beyond making a profit.

Values: how we operate...the standards we commit to operating by.

Vision: an expression of what team members want the organization to become.

Goals: what the team must achieve in the short term to achieve the Vision.

Procedures: the specific steps the team must execute to achieve the goals.

Roles/Responsibilities: what each team member must do.

Communication: clear, concise, and consistent communication.

Earlier I mentioned a responsibility-based culture. Let us examine the differences between a responsibility-based culture and an authoritarian-based culture.

Shifting from Authority-driven to Responsibility-based Work Cultures

In our business culture, there has been a lot of discussion about a shift away from the old-school "command and control" style to more collaborative approaches. With Magnetic Leadership, we are creating a responsibility-based organization versus an authoritatively driven organization.

Cultural Differences[viii]

	Responsibility-based	Authority-driven
Level of trust	Trust is essential and at a high level. Managers and employees focus on being trustworthy and building trust.	Trust is limited. It is difficult to trust people who avoid responsibility or have control over you.
Leadership behavior	Leaders believe in people. They partner with employees to create a great organization.	Managers use rules and procedures, performance appraisals and incentives to ensure compliance.
Responsibility and accountability	Everyone takes responsibility, works together to solve problems and takes ownership of the outcome.	No one wants to accept responsibility. They stick to the rules and blame others for mistakes.
Employee behavior	Self-directed people are responsible, creative and use initiative. They take ownership of their jobs.	Other-directed people do what people tell them to do, avoid taking risks, use no initiative, and some rebel.

When you read the differences, the attitude is almost palpable. Which organization do you want to work for? Which one do you want to lead?

What Will the Results Look Like When Your Organization Gets There?

Here is what you will see in a culture built on trust:

1. **Responsibility and accountability are high.**
2. **Individuals accept change initiatives.**
3. **People choose to go above and beyond.**
4. **People think outside of their roles and responsibilities.**
5. **Individuals accept responsibility for their actions.**
6. **Individuals feel accepted and respected.**

Resurrect Those Gold Stars

Buy yourself a package of gold stars—big ones—similar to the ones your teacher used to put on your spelling test. As you build trust in your organization, place a gold star next to each of the signs you see growing in your organization. It will bring you back to the place of pride you felt long ago, and it generally sparks a smile in even the most cynical of us.

In chapter one, we looked at vision, purpose and values, and the role they play in leadership. We also explored the importance of trust as a foundation for your leadership and introduced you to the R.E.A.L. approach. Before we get R.E.A.L., let us look at your own leadership style.

Chapter Two
People Follow an Authentic Leader

> *"Just as a compass points toward a magnetic field, your True North pulls you toward the purpose of your leadership. When you follow your internal compass, your leadership will be authentic, and people will naturally want to associate with you. Although others may guide or influence you, your truth is derived from your life story and only you can determine what it should be."*
>
> **—Bill George, with Peter Sims, Authors of True North**

Where Do You Stand?

To be a Magnetic Leader you also need to be authentic.

Authentic Leadership[iv] is:

- Being the real you.

- Finding coherence between your life story and your leadership.

- Bringing people together around a shared purpose.

- Empowering people to step up and create value.

Knowing yourself is:

- Finding the passion that motivates you.

- Finding the purpose of your leadership.

- Feeling comfortable in your own skin.

- Knowing your strengths and weaknesses and filling the skill gaps with colleagues that complement you.

- Seeing yourself as others see you.

Dianne M. Durkin with Carey Earle

What kind of a leader are you? Are you people-oriented or task-oriented? Participative or authoritarian? This chapter offers you several self-assessments that can help you answer questions about where you stand as a leader. At the end of the chapter, there are more tools to help you as you chart your journey as a leader.

Let us begin by taking the task-oriented assessment from Andrew Dubrin's "Leadership, Research Findings, Practice and Skills."[x]

People-oriented vs. Task-oriented Assessment

This self-assessment tool[xi] looks at whether you are more people oriented or task oriented. Use the key below as you answer the questions.

N = Never
S = Seldom
O = Occasionally
F = Frequently
A = Always

1. I would most likely act as the spokesperson of the group.   N S O F A

2. I would encourage overtime work.   N S O F A

3. I would allow members complete freedom in their work.   N S O F A

4. I would encourage the use of uniform procedures.   N S O F A

5. I would permit the members to use their own judgment in solving problems.   N S O F A

6. I would stress being ahead of competing groups.   N S O F A

7. I would speak as a representative of the group.   N S O F A

8. I would needle members for greater effort.   N S O F A

9. I would try out my ideas in the group.   N S O F A

10. I would let the members do their work the way they think best.   N S O F A

11. I would be working hard for a promotion.   N S O F A

12. I would be able to tolerate postponement and   N S O F A
    uncertainty.

13. I would speak for the group when visitors were present.   N S O F A

14. I would keep the work moving at a rapid pace.   N S O F A

15. I would turn the members loose on a job and let   N S O F A
    them go to it.

16. I would settle conflicts when they occur in the group.   N S O F A

17. I would get swamped by details.   N S O F A

18. I would represent the group at outside meetings.   N S O F A

19. I would be reluctant to allow the members any   N S O F A
    freedom of action.

20. I would decide what to do and how to do it.   N S O F A

21. I would push for increased production.   N S O F A

22. I would let some members have authority that I   N S O F A
    should keep.

23. Things would usually turn out as I predict.   N S O F A

24. I would allow the group a high degree of initiative.   N S O F A

25. I would assign group members particular tasks.   N S O F A

26. I would be willing to make changes.   N S O F A

27. I would ask members to work harder.   N S O F A

28. I would trust the group members to exercise good   N S O F A
    judgment.

29. I would schedule the work.   N S O F A

30. I would refuse to explain my actions.   N S O F A

31. I would persuade others that my ideas are to their advantage.   N S O F A

32. I would permit the group to set its own pace.   N S O F A

33. I would urge the group to beat its previous record.   N S O F A

34. I would act without consulting the group.   N S O F A

35. I would ask that group members follow standard rules and regulations.   N S O F A

What is Your Score?

- Circle the numbers 8, 12, 17, 18, 19, 20, 34 and 35.

- Write the number 1 in front of the circled numbers if you responded S or N.

- Write a number 1 in front of the numbers not circled if you responded A or F.

- Circle the number 1s that you have written in front of the following items: 3, 5, 8, 10, 15, 18, 19, 22, 24, 26, 28, 30, 32, 34 and 35.

- Count the circled number 1s. This is your people-oriented score. A 7 is high.

- Count the uncircled number 1s. This is your task-oriented score. A 10 is high.

There is no right or wrong answer. What matters here is your self-awareness. For example, if you score high as a task-oriented leader, you may need to focus more on the people and make sure you do not come across as a task master. If you are more people oriented, you may need to focus more on getting the job done. Understanding how people perceive you is an important part of leadership. You can only be authentic when your view of yourself aligns with the world around you.

A R.E.A.L. Tip

What is important is your own self-awareness as a leader. If you scored high, you may need to "turn down the volume," and make sure your emotions are not threatening to others.

If you scored too low, then think about a friend or colleague you perceive as a very expressive and charismatic person. Watch and note what you could do to hit the right chord.

What Style of Leader Are You or Would You Be?[xii]

Are you more participative or authoritarian? As you answer the following questions, think about what you have done or would do in the scenarios and attitudes described. Write MT for Mostly True of MF for Mostly False for each question.

Mostly True = **MT**   Mostly False = **MF**

1. I am more likely to take care of a high-impact assignment myself than turn it over to a group member.   ____ ____

2. I would prefer the analytical aspects of a manager's job to working directly with group members.   ____ ____

3. An important part of my approach to managing a group is to keep the members informed almost daily of any information that could affect their work.   ____ ____

4. It is a good idea to give two people in the group the same problem and then choose what appears to be the best solution.   ____ ____

5. It makes good sense for the leader or manager to stay somewhat aloof from the group so you can make a tough decision when necessary.

Dianne M. Durkin with Carey Earle

6. I look for opportunities to obtain group input before making a decision, even on straightforward issues.   _____ _____

7. I would reverse a decision if several of the group members presented evidence that I was wrong.   _____ _____

8. Differences of opinion in the work group are healthy.   _____ _____

9. I think activities to build team spirit, like fixing up a poor family's home on a Saturday, are an excellent investment of time.   _____ _____

10. If my group were hiring a new member, I would like the entire group to interview the person.   _____ _____

11. An effective team leader today uses e-mail for about 98 percent of communication with team members.   _____ _____

12. Some of the best ideas are likely to come from the group members rather than from the manager.   _____ _____

13. If our group was going to have a banquet, I would get input from each member on what type of food to serve.   _____ _____

14. I have never seen a statue of a committee in a museum or park, so why bother making decisions by committee if you want to be recognized.   _____ _____

15. I dislike it intensely when a group member challenges my position on an issue.   _____ _____

16. I typically explain to group members how (what method) to accomplish an assigned task.   _____ _____

17. If I were out of the office for a week, the group would accomplish most of the important work anyway.   _____ _____

18. Delegation of important tasks is something that would be (or is) very difficult for me.   _____ _____

19. When a group member comes to me with a problem, I tend to jump right in with a solution.   _____ _____

20. When a group member comes to me with a problem, ____ ____
I typically ask that person something like, "What
alternative solutions have you thought of so far?"

These are the answers for a participative leader:

1. Mostly False	8. Mostly True	15. Mostly False
2. Mostly False	9. Mostly True	16. Mostly False
3. Mostly True	10. Mostly True	17. Mostly True
4. Mostly False	11. Mostly False	18. Mostly False
5. Mostly False	12. Mostly True	19. Mostly False
6. Mostly True	13. Mostly True	20. Mostly True
7. Mostly True	14. Mostly False	

For each of your answers that match the ones above, give yourself a point. If your score is 15 or higher, you are most likely a participative leader. If your score is 5 or lower, you are most likely an authoritarian leader.

When you look at the statements, you can see cues to a more participative leadership style. For example, in statement 12 it says: "Some of the best ideas are likely to come from the group members rather than from the manager." If this is mostly true for you as a leader, it means you are willing to listen and encourage input from others. You recognize you cannot know everything about a given situation.

In question 16, the cue is different: "If you are continually telling people how to approach a particular situation, you are not allowing people to be creative, think and learn for themselves." This tends to be an authoritative style. Review all the questions and make a list of things you want to change about your style. Magnetic Leaders, as we will discover, ask, listen and engage people. They allow them to bring their brains to work and think of alternative solutions.

Six Managerial Styles: What Rings True?

In the chart on the next page are the six managerial styles[xiii] that require different emotional strengths and that often work best in certain situations. For example, an authoritative approach mobilizes people toward a vision and can be a powerful leadership style when change is required.

As you read through the chart below, ask yourself these key questions:

- Which words do I identify with most and do I hear myself often saying?

- Which emotional competencies do I have?

- What style best aligns with where my organization is right now and where it needs to go?

What Rings True?	Modus operandi	The style in a phrase	Emotional intelligence competencies	When the style works best	Overall impact on climate
Coercive	Demands immediate compliance.	"Do what I tell you."	Drive to achieve, initiative, self-control.	In a crisis, to kick-start a turnaround, or with problem employees.	Negative
Authoritative	Mobilizes people toward a vision.	"Come with me."	Self-confidence, empathy, change catalyst.	When changes require a new vision, or when a clear direction is needed.	Most strongly positive
Affiliative	Creates harmony and builds an emotional bond.	"People come first."	Empathy, building relationships, communication.	To heal rifts in a team or to motivate people during stressful circumstances.	Positive
Democratic	Forges consensus through participation.	"What do you think?"	Collaboration, team leadership, communication.	To build buy-in or consensus, or to get input from valuable employees.	Positive
Pacesetting	Sets high standards for performance.	"Do as I do, now!"	Conscientiousness, drive to achieve, initiative.	To get quick results from a highly motivated and competent team.	Negative
Coaching	Develops people for the future.	"Try this."	Developing others, empathy, self-awareness.	To help an employee improve performance or develop long-term strengths.	Positive

Just as in the previous assessments regarding people- and task-oriented, and participative and authoritarian leadership styles – you need to balance the six managerial styles described here based upon the situation. Flexibility is one of the most important characteristics of a Magnetic Leader. Let us determine how flexible you are.

How Flexible Are You?

Regardless of what managerial style you use in a given situation, in a world where change is a norm, you need to be flexible. Answer the questions[xiv] below to test your flexibility.

Answer "often," "sometimes" or "rarely" to the following questions.

1. Do you tend to seek out only those people who agree with your analysis of issues?

2. Do you ignore most of the advice from coworkers about process improvements?

3. Do your team members go along with what you say just to avoid an argument?

4. Have people referred to you as "rigid" or "close minded" on several occasions?

5. When presented with a new method, do you immediately look for a flaw?

6. Do you make up your mind early on with respect to an issue, and then hold firmly to your opinion?

7. When people disagree with you, do you tend to belittle them or become argumentative?

8. Do you often feel you are the only person in the group who really understands the problem?

How Did You Score?

If you answered "rarely" to seven or eight questions, you are unusually adaptable. If you answered "sometimes" to at least five questions, you are on the right track and should focus on more flexibility to help you grow your leadership skills. If you answered "often" to more than four questions, you have a long way to go to improve your flexibility and adaptability. However, your honesty is the first critical step to improvement.

Next, let us look at your personal magnetism and how it might be affecting your career path.

The Personal Magnetism Deficit Inventory[xv]

Is a lack of personal magnetism holding your career back and keeping you from being the leader you could be?

Five Ways to Increase your Personal Magnetism

1. Inspire people with your vision. People want to think about the future and possibilities. If you have a window into where the organization is going, share it.

2. Ignite people with your energy. Energy and enthusiasm are contagious. If you walk into a room tired and frustrated, you can bring the energy down, and people remember you as the person who is a killjoy.

3. Get things done. Be seen as a leader who empowers people to get things done, and who asks: "Why not?"

4. Remember people. People feel good and special when others remember them. Come up with ways to remember people's names. It can be coming up with a visual that reminds you of the person's name or maybe a rhyme. Anything that works for you to conjure up names quickly.

5. Be candid and authentic. People like to be around leaders who "tell it like it is." When you are confident, you can cut to the heart of the matter and be candid. People respect that quality and feel included when you share what is on your mind.

Now that I have you all pumped up with personal magnetism, let me turn the volume down so you can listen to all the important cues that surround you every minute.

Are You a Leader Who Listens?

One of things your customers and employees want is for someone to hear them. They want to know someone is listening. As a leader, you do not want your team to see you as someone who is just waiting to talk and therefore never listening to what others say.

Ten questions to test your listening skills

1. Do you half-listen to what people say?

2. Do you make assumptions regarding what the person meant to say?

3. Do you jump to conclusions before the person has finished speaking?

4. Are you eager to talk about what you think?

5. Do you agree before you have heard in full what the person wanted to say?

6. Do you interrupt frequently?

7. Do you finish other people's sentences?

8. Do you take so many notes that you lose the meaning of what people say and are not reading the room or making sufficient eye contact?

9. Do you judge others as they are speaking?

10. Do you multi-task when someone is talking to you either in person or on the phone?

If you answered yes to more than three of these questions, you could be demoralizing the people around you by simply not listening to them. Listening is a powerful signal. In chapter three, I talk in detail about effective listening and its role in Magnetic Leadership.

Your Leadership Intentions

Now that you have a better picture of where you stand as a leader, what are your intentions? Think about what you would like to accomplish and in what time frame?

_____

_____

_____

What do you want to hold yourself accountable for as a leader?

_____

_____

_____

What are the leadership traits you are really good at?

_____

_____

_____

What are the leadership skills you want to work on?

_____

_____

_____

_____

What support will you need to achieve the above?

_____

_____

_____

_____

Also, think about the impact of each of your goals. Which ones are critical to the growth and success of your organization? Prioritize the leadership goals you think are most important to your success and that of your team.

_____

_____

_____

_____

Your 21-Day Leadership Log

Once you have your leadership goals and you have increased your own self-awareness about your leadership style, you will begin to notice things you did not notice before.

You will have some "Ahas!" And you will want to write those down.

You will also see some of your leadership at work, and you will want to write down what is working well and what additional changes you would like to make.

Finally, you will come up with ideas – often when you are not working, and you will want to be sure to capture those gems!

To keep track of this information, I suggest keeping a leadership log. It becomes a physical manifestation of your journey as a leader, showing your own growth and discoveries along the way!

Reflecting on your leadership style

Keeping a Leadership Journal for 21 days can and will change behaviors. Alcoholics Anonymous, Weight Watchers and many other organizations recognize that documenting behavior for 21-consecutive days changes behavior and actions.

Use the Leadership Log on the next page for 21 days, and see the magnetic changes it creates in you and with your people.

21- Day Leadership Log
Reflecting on Your Leadership Style

What leadership traits did I exhibit today?

_____

_____

_____

Was I flexible? Did I adjust my style to work more effectively with others?

_____

_____

_____

How have I built my trust bank with others?

_____

_____

_____

Did I stop and listen versus react?

_____

_____

_____

_____

What was my modus operandi, and was it appropriate for the situation?

_____

_____

_____

_____

You now have a better understanding of yourself as a leader; you have set some leadership goals, have the tools to help you capture your leadership lessons and ideas, and are in the right frame of mind to get R.E.A.L. So, let us start at the beginning with the letter R.

Chapter Three
Make it "Right" and Get Results

> *"The best executive is the one who has sense enough*
> *to pick good men to do what he wants done, and self restraint*
> *enough to keep from meddling with them when they do it."*
>
> **—Theodore Roosevelt**

In order to build that culture of leadership I discussed in chapters one and two, you have to recruit the right people in the right places at the right times. You also need to retain them. Sounds simple, and yet as I speak with leaders across the globe, organizations continually struggle to ensure they have the right talent addressing the business issues at hand. It all begins with the interviewing process.

When I ask leaders what makes someone successful in their organizations, I regularly hear the following characteristics:

- Flexibility.
- Passion and enthusiasm.
- Optimism.
- Listening and questioning mindset.
- Humility.
- Independent learner.
- Able to deal with chaos and change.
- Outside-the-box thinker
- Multitasker.
- Team player.

Notice there is very little mention of particular skills. It is more about the attitude and personal attributes of the candidates. So the big question is – how do you hire for these characteristics?

Without the right tools and techniques, we so often default to common recruiting errors. We have all done it. Any of these sound familiar?

- Talking too much about the organization.

- Not listening to the applicant because we are thinking of the next question to ask.

- Hiring someone who is just like you.

- Hiring the person because we have to fill the position now.

- Recruiting only for the position and not for values that fit in the culture.

If you are going to recruit the right people at the right time and in the right place, here are some things you have to focus on when you are hiring:

Culture. This is the first and most important thing. Think about the characteristics of the people who thrive in your organization. Are they flexible, passionate, independent and humble? Or are they questioning innovators who find new ways to solve problems? If the employees you are hiring do not match your culture, they will not succeed—which is a colossal waste of everyone's time and resources.

Attitude is second most important. There are many things we can teach. Attitude is not one of them. Turning a pessimist into an optimist is often a futile exercise. Instead, you want to hire people who are "positive on life," self-directed and who are accountable and responsible for their actions.

You want to hire people who look at the glass as half full, not half empty. We have all heard those words, so let us think about them in the context of interviewing. When people are "positive on life," they believe they create their lives with every thought. They recognize anything is possible if they focus on the goal. And, with that focus, the right people and things show up in their lives at the right time. It is all about the Law of Attraction as popularized by Rhonda Byrne in her international bestseller, "The Secret."

Self-directed people make choices and accept the consequences of their choices. These are the people who, when they are wrong, own up to it, accept responsibility **and** are accountable for their actions.

Other-directed people wait for someone to tell them what to do. They do not feel responsible for their actions and often are very good at playing the "blame game" and feeling like a victim.

Competence. Make sure you involve the right people in the interview process, so you can really drill down on all areas of competence from communication and management skills to technical skills.

How do you know you are hitting the right notes in an interview? You need an interview process that asks the right questions, looks for the right skills and teaches your interviewers to listen for revealing answers. If your process is too complex, people will push it aside and go back to business as usual. It has to be accessible, and your managers need to clearly see the value. Let us take a look at a Four-Step Interview Process and think about how this would work in your organization to help you recruit the right people.

Four-Step Team Interview Process

We are all human, and we all have a bias about the people we like and want to work with. The best way to account for that bias is to have a team of interviewers with different roles in the interview process.

1. **Opener**

    The first person in the interview process is the opener. This person introduces the company and the position and focuses on:

    - Why the candidate is interested in the company?

    - Why the candidate is interested in the position?

    - Why the candidate is leaving their present position?

    - Is the candidate a good cultural fit with the company?

2. **Hard-skills interviewer**

    The second part of the interview process focuses on the technical skills, or "hard skills," needed for the position. In this step, you should have at least two interviewers who clearly understand the job-skill requirements and can probe very specifically from different perspectives. Guide them to focus on:

    - Specific qualifications for the position, such as certifications or software/hardware knowledge that is critical.

    - What major accomplishments has the interviewee achieved?

    - How does the interviewee handle challenges in his position?

    - How does this candidate learn new things?

- How does this candidate solve problems?

- Can the candidate demonstrate project management skills?

- What has the candidate done to continue to enhance his professional development?

3. Soft-skills interviewer

The third part of the interview process focuses on communication skills, work ethic, adaptability, ability to work on a team and customer-relationship skills. Guide this interviewer to focus on the following:

- What is the level of the candidate's written, oral and presentation skills?

- How effectively does the person work on a team?

- Is the person best at self-management/individual contributor, team management/senior contributor or project management?

- How does the candidate handle risk management?

- How does the candidate handle stress and change? How flexible and adaptable is the person?

- How successful is the person in building relationships inside and outside the organization? Can the person demonstrate sensitivity and urgency?

- What problem-solving skills does the candidate have?

4. Closer

The closer is generally a human resources manager or a hiring manager. Before this interview, the closer has gathered input from all interviewers and enters this final phase with a strong overall picture of the candidate.

If the feedback from the other interviewers has been positive, the closer will probe on any open issues, sell the organization, answer questions and also try to ascertain what other offers or opportunities the candidate is reviewing.

If the feedback from the other interviewers was negative, the closer ends the interview process as soon as possible.

Getting the Best Information

We have all been on many interviews, and when the interview is predictable, we know what to say and what not to say. For example, who is going to say they are NOT a team player when asked if they work well as part of a team?

The key of good interviewing and gathering the information highlighted in this chapter is to ask questions that allow the candidates to reveal who they truly are. A good technique is to use different types of questions to illicit different responses. Here are three types of questions to use:

Three types of questions

1. **Open-ended questions are for gathering information**

    - Start with: What/Why/How/Tell me about.

    - Example: What happened with this project? Tell me about…

    - Note: "Why" questions are about concepts. "How" questions are about process. "What" questions are about information.

2. **Close-ended questions are for guiding the discussion and getting details**

    - Start with: Is, Have, Do, Are, Will, Could, When, Where, Who

    - Example: When did you start and end the project?
      How long did it take you to complete the project?
      Which software are you most proficient with?

3. **High-impact questions are for getting the other person's commitment.**

    - Start with: What effect does that have on…?
      How does that cause…?
      What does that result in…?

    - Example: What impact did your decision have on the overall project?
      What effect did you have on the overall project?
      What would you avoid in the future?

Use all of these questions to meet your interviewing objectives. Remember, a combination of questions manages the conversation and lets candidates reveal themselves. In interviewing, it is good to remember we have two ears and one mouth, which is nature's way of reminding us we should listen twice as much as we talk!

A R.E.A.L. Tip

Use "How" questions to focus on process. Use "What" questions to gather information. Use "Why" questions sparingly. They can put a person on the defensive. At the same time, they can be effective in trying to learn about a particular concept such as: "Why do you believe...?" or "Why do you think...?"

Questioning strategy

A leader's secret weapon is questions. Using a systematic approach to questions creates a questioning strategy. Effective questioning strategies help candidates feel comfortable and ultimately provide invaluable information about the candidate.

Inverted Pyramid Approach to Questioning

I have found that the inverted pyramid is a good framework to use as you develop your own questioning strategy. It shows interviewers the flow to use in interviewing, beginning with background questions, then moving on to methodology questions, detail questions and ending with lessons learned.

Throughout this flow, I recommend people use open-ended and high-impact questions and limit the use of close-ended questions. It is important to remember that as interviewers, we need to allow the candidate to express himself. When you do so, you will be amazed at what you will learn.

Let us look at how a hard-skills interviewer and soft-skills interviewer use the inverted-pyramid approach to support their objectives. (See the examples chart below.)

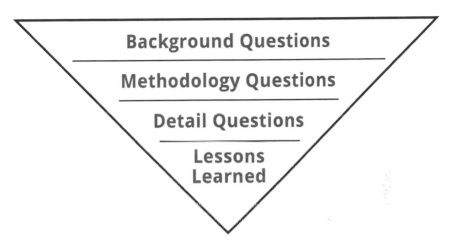

Background questions

Use them to encourage people to describe a situation and give you a clearer picture of what motivates them.

Examples:

Hard-skills Interviewer	Soft-skills Interviewer
What was the best project you ever worked on? What made it such a great project?	What role do you usually play in a team environment?
What was the most challenging project you ever worked on?	On a project you worked on, please describe the interactions you had?

Methodology questions

These questions create a common understanding of what the person has done to resolve a problem and how the problem resolution impacted the business.

Examples:

Hard-skills Interviewer	Soft-skills Interviewer
Would you describe a challenging situation you encountered and how you resolved it?	What would you have done if your manager said he was going to have to cut the staff and time frame on the your project?
What was the impact of your efforts on the project?	How would you handle a staffing reduction with your team?

Detail questions

When you want to gather more specific information or background information from previous questions, you can uncover the details with these questions.

Examples:

Hard-skills Interviewer	Soft-skills Interviewer
What, specifically, went right/ wrong with the situation you described?	What do you try to avoid in interactions?
How did you recover from it?	When you encounter a challenge, how do you approach it?

Lessons learned

Use these questions to identify, assign and gain information about learning capabilities and other characteristics.

Examples:

Hard-skills Interviewer	Soft-skills Interviewer
What would you do differently to avoid this situation in the future?	What would you have done differently on this project with your team, customer, or partners?
What did you learn from this situation?	Would you work with the same team again and why?
How did this project fit into the overall product strategy?	How would you apply what you learned to future projects?

Notice all the questions are open ended. Open-ended questions allow the candidate to fully describe the situation and provide you the opportunity to learn much more about candidates and their qualifications

Uncovering the Candidate's Criteria

When we become involved in the interview process, it is easy to forget we are not the only one doing the evaluation. We have to remember the candidates are also evaluating us and our company. They have their own criteria that they want met. Using the interview process to uncover their important criteria can reduce misconceptions and misunderstandings in the future.

First, let us make sure we are using the same definition of criteria. In this case, criteria are the values and standards a person is applying to a particular situation. What is important, special, right, wrong, good, bad, desirable, or undesirable for that person?

You can learn this by asking candidates, "What questions do you have for me?" Their first question provides you with an indication of what is of prime importance to them. Listen to those first questions carefully, and then ask additional ones to clarify and gather more information.

Question

For example, if the first question is: "What does your benefits plan consist of?" you may want to follow up with the following questions:

Answers and/or responses

- "What is important to you about the benefits program?"

- "Tell me more about why that is of primary importance to you."

You may discover the person has a family member with a health issue and health benefits are important to that candidate's peace of mind.

Question

Another question the candidate may ask is: "What is the culture of the organization?"

Answer and/or response

- "What type of culture do you find you work best in?"

To complete this segment of the interview, you need to provide candidates with input as to how their criteria fit or do not fit the culture of your organization. When describing culture, your honesty is key. Here is an example to illustrate what I mean.

I recently interviewed a candidate who was extremely well qualified for the position, had all the right motivations to make a cross country move and seemed like he would really fit into the culture of the company. When I asked if he had any questions, he asked about the management styles of two senior members of the team. When I asked if he had some concerns, his response said it all. "My perception is that these two individuals manage very differently, and I am going to have to work very closely with both of them."

To clarify, I said, "Please tell me more." His response was, "I hate to be micromanaged."

I clearly knew that one of the individuals had control/micromanagement tendencies. With additional questions, the candidate and I were able to further investigate his description of micromanagement and develop strategies on how he could best work with this senior person.

All this happened in the interview process. Can you imagine how much time and energy this saved? Be totally honest with your candidates. If the company cannot meet their expectations of management styles – tell them. If things really need fixing, and you need their expertise, tell them. When you paint a pretty picture in the interview process, you risk losing that person within a short period of time at great expense to the company.

Here is another example that showcases the importance of the interview portraying reality versus an idyllic version of the job.

A company hired an individual without knowing the expectations of his manager and without the true management style of the person he would be working for coming through in the interview. Six weeks into the job, that individual handed in his resignation. In the exit interview, he said, "Two weeks into the job I knew my manager's style and mine would not work, and I did not want that pressure and stress, so I decided to start looking for another position using the existing network I set up during my initial job search."

Communication, honesty and straightforwardness are the pillars of Magnetic Leadership.

Question

If the interviewee asks: "What is the decision-making process in the organization?"

Answer and/or response

- "Tell me more about the type of decision-making process you work best with?"

- Once you elicit a response you may want to delve more deeply by asking, "What does having that type of decision-making process do for you?"

Here are additional questions that can uncover a candidate's criteria

- What is important to you about…?

- Tell me more…

- What would having that do for you?

- What is your concern about?

- What would you rather have or prefer?

Think of questions as your "Secret Weapons." Open-ended and high-impact questions bring out the true qualities of the candidate. Remember to begin questions with "what," "how" and "would you describe…" As I mentioned previously, I encourage interviewers to limit "why" questions as they can create defensive responses. How do you feel when you read the questions below?

"Why did you…?"
"Why did you ask that?"
"Why do you feel that way?"

If you feel a candidate getting defensive, that is the normal reaction to "why" questions.

A R.E.A.L. Tip

People love to talk. Ask questions that allow candidates to describe situations, themselves and their own criteria. When given the opportunity, people will reveal themselves.

Checking in with Checkpoint Summaries

Throughout the interview process, you want to ensure both you and the candidate have a mutual understanding of the position, expectations, roles and responsibilities and the cultural dynamics of the organization.

Checkpoint summaries help you make sure you are capturing and communicating all the important information you need to make good hiring decisions. They allow you to restate what you have heard, clarify any misconceptions and gain additional information in a non-threatening manner.

Examples of some checkpoint summaries:

- I heard that the type of environment you work best in is _____.
  What other things are important to you about the kind of environment you thrive in?

- Based upon what you have told me, I sense you are an overachiever. What do you do to relax?

- Earlier in the interview, you mentioned some of the first things you would do if we offered you this position. Are there any other things you would do?

- Are we in agreement that if we were to offer you the position, you would like the following training _____ prior to assuming full responsibility? Are there any other things you believe you would like to do to better prepare yourself for the responsibilities of this position?

Your interviewer checklist

Like so many things in being a Magnetic Leader, planning is critical. The interview process is no exception. Before any interview, it is important to review the résumé or CV of the person you are interviewing so you have a basic understanding of her achievements and can prepare your questions. It also is important to be clear on what you need to know by the end of the interview. Use each of the different kinds of questions to guide you and help you to acquire the best information from each candidate. Some of my favorite questions are below. See how you might incorporate these into your interview style and into the questioning strategy we described in this chapter.

Some favorite questions

- What would you hope this résumé says about you?

- What was an extremely challenging situation you encountered in your life and how did you handle it?

- In the brief time I have spoken with you, I am sure there are numerous things I have not learned. If we were to hire you, what additional information should I know about you?

- What additional things should I know about you that I have not thought to ask?

- What are the top three things that are the most important to you in a position?

Take some time now to develop your interviewing questions:

Background

Encourage people to describe a situation and give you a clearer picture of what motivates them.

_____

_____

Methodology

Create a common understanding of what the person has done to resolve a problem and how the problem resolution impacted the business.

_____

_____

Detail

Gather more specific information or background info from previous questions. Get down to the details.

_____

_____

Lessons learned

Identify, assign and gain information on how the person has grown from prior experiences.

_____

_____

Criteria

Ascertain the values and standards a candidate will apply to a particular situation.

_____

_____

Getting Your Ears in the Game

You now know how to effectively ask questions during an interview. That is half the battle. The other half is knowing how to listen. Let us determine how good a listener you are.

Listening skills self-evaluation[xvi]

Use the following assessment to determine a sense of what is important to you when communicating with others. Think about how often you do the following and write in the number you believe matches that frequency. Use the scale below.

1 = Never   **3** = Sometimes   **5** = Very often
2 = Rarely   **4** = Often

Behavior	Score
I remain open to hearing the rest of the other person's message even after she presents ideas with which I disagree.	
I ask the other person to repeat or clarify a point I don't fully understand.	
I listen for an overall theme behind the person's message.	
I do not try to fix the situation before trying to understand it.	
I try not to judge someone's message based on what I think of her as a person.	
I place more importance on what the person is communicating rather than how the person is communicating.	
I offer a summary of the other person's main ideas at the end of the conversation.	
Total Score: Add up your score in the column to the right. A higher score indicates more active and effective listening.	

Dianne M. Durkin with Carey Earle

While listening is critical, it also is really important to be present during an interview and to pay attention to the cues your candidate gives you in both verbal and non-verbal communication. Think about the three components of communication: body language, voice and words. Which of these do you believe has the largest impact in face-to-face communications? The answers may surprise you.

1. Physiology (body language)   **55 percent**
2. Voice (volume/pace)   **38 percent**
3. Words   **7 percent**

During in-person communications, body language represents 55 percent of our communication, voice (volume, pace, pitch, tone) is 38 percent and only 7 percent is the words. Simply put—it is not what you say; it is how you say it.

In an interview situation, a person's body language can relate any discomfort over certain aspects of the job, philosophies of the company or the culture. Watch for body language changes that may reflect these discomforts.

Although words are only 7 percent of the communications and 38 percent is voice, by listening very carefully you can detect sub-messages or emotions. Let us look at this more closely by examining Steven Covey's five levels of listening.

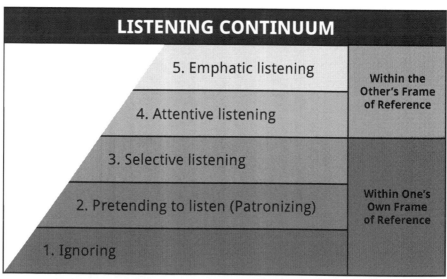

Source: The 8th Habit: From Effectiveness to Greatness. Stephen Covey. Free Press, a division of Simon & Schuster. New York, NY. 2004.

The first three—Ignoring, Pretending and Selective listening—are all within our own frame of reference. They are all about us. Attentive listening and Empathetic listening are in the other person's frame of reference. With attentive and empathetic listening we are truly seeking to understand both the content and the emotions of the other person.

How Are We Communicating?

Ignoring—You are not present and telling the person they are not important.

Pretending—Giving the person the impression you are listening.

Selective listening—Spurts, words and information important to me.

Attentive listening—Attentive to words and content the other person is trying to communicate.

Empathetic listening—Understanding the feelings and emotions of the other person.

Let us look more closely at attentive and empathetic listening. How do you make sure you spend most of your time at the higher end of the spectrum?

How to become an empathetic listener

Empathetic listening is the highest level of listening. An emphatic listener is someone who is listening beyond the words to identify feelings, intentions and implications of what the other person is saying. You are listening for what the person says as well as what he does not say.

An empathetic listener is careful not to make assumptions. Rather, they are working to understand and to clarify. For example, an empathetic listener might ask:

"It sounds like meeting deadlines is important to you. Can you tell me about some deadlines you have had to achieve?" or "I am sensing you are not fully comfortable with the decision we just made."

In an interview situation, you can also link what you are hearing to test a solution. For example, with our candidate who values deadlines, you might ask: "If you had a project due with half the time required, how would you handle the deadlines?"

Attentive listening

If we are only listening to the words, we are only hearing part of the story. As an attentive listener, you focus on the words and content. When you combine attentive with empathetic listening, you are watching the body language, listening to the voice and paying attention to the meaning and emotions beneath the words.

Attentive and empathetic listening helps you to:

- Gain deeper insights into the real situation.

- Override the judgments we may make.

- Take the time to validate the feelings and intentions of others.

- Create a sense of respect for the other people.

- Establish a stronger connection with people.

A R.E.A.L. Tip

Ask yourself: When other people are talking, am I preparing my response instead of listening to what they are saying? Or perhaps I am thinking about the next question I am going to ask versus listening for emotions.

Empathetic Listening in Motion

Think of an interview situation you face regularly and how you could use attentive and empathetic listening to identify the feelings, intentions and implications in that situation. Then, link what you heard to a question that could drive to a constructive solution.

Example:

YOU: Why are looking to leave your current position?

MARY: I am so tired of the lack of teamwork there. No one cares, and it is really exhausting. I am ready for a new environment.

YOU: It sounds like you are not feeling supported by your team, and you want people to pitch in. Is that a fair assessment?

MARY: Exactly, I just want other people to do their part.

YOU: If you were leading the team, what would you do differently to attain the kind of teamwork you would like?

The empathetic listener is not judging Mary's response. The listener is, instead, hearing and acknowledging the candidate's frustration and then providing the opportunity for her to link that frustration to a potential solution.

This allows you to see what kind of a thinker Mary is by allowing her the opportunity to express any solutions she might have. You also can see if Mary is someone who only complains versus providing constructive ideas.

Ten Dos and Don'ts of Listening

Dos	Don'ts
1. Be patient.	Don't half listen, filter or selectively listen.
2. Take brief notes of key points.	Don't make assumptions regarding what the person meant to say.
3. Offer verbal encouragement.	Don't jump to conclusions.
4. Read between the lines for emotional messages.	Don't be too eager to talk about your recommendation.
5. Allow for periods of silence.	Don't agree too readily when you have not heard the person out.
6. Let the person speaking complete his thought.	Don't interrupt.
7. Ask questions to clarify understanding.	Don't finish the other person's sentences.
8. Choose to understand the person by looking for their feelings and good intentions.	Don't take so many notes that you lose the meaning of the dialogue.
9. Summarize what you both said or covered.	Don't judge the other person.
10. Assume you have not understood everything correctly.	Don't complete other tasks while you are listening to the person on the phone or in person.

Understanding Who You Are Talking To

Another huge benefit of attentive listening is you can learn the communication preferences of other people and communicate with them more effectively. Let me explain.

Sixty percent of the population has a visual preference for communication and learning, and uses visual verbs.

You hear them say:

"Your approach is not **clear** to me..."

"This data doesn't **look** right..."

"I do not **see** your point..."

"That does not clearly **show** that..."

"I cannot seem to **focus** on what you are saying..."

Twenty percent of people have an auditory preference for communication and learning, and use auditory verbs

You hear them say:

"That does not **sound** right..."

"**Tell** me about that approach..."

"You **told** me that..."

"What exactly are you **saying**..."

"That is more **noise** than substance..."

"What you are **saying** does not seem to **click** with me..."

Twenty percent of people have an emotional or kinesthetic preference for communication and learning, and use feeling verbs.

You hear them say:

"That does not **feel** right..."

"I have a **gut** feeling that..."

"I am **uncomfortable** with…"

"Why are you **pushing** this…"

"I just do not **like** the way you are doing…"

When you are talking with someone, and you hear these cues, you want to respond in kind. Basically, you are speaking his language in the true human sense of the word.

When you hear visual cues, you can respond like this

"Let me **clarify** that for you…"

"Let me **show** you where the problem is…"

"Here is a different way to **look** at it…"

"What is your **perspective** on the situation?"

"Let me **see** if I can pinpoint this…"

When you hear auditory cues, you can respond like this

"Let me **say** it in a different way…"

"How do these next steps **sound**?"

"Let me **restate** what I meant…"

"If that **sounds** confusing, let me explain…"

"I hear you. Let me try to **explain** it differently."

When you hear feeling cues, you can respond like this

"Let me **guide you** through the steps…"

"Let us **develop** a plan you can live with…"

"Let me **set you at ease** with this approach…"

"What can I do to make you **feel more comfortable**?"

"Would a **hands-on demo** work better for you?"

When you respond visual to visual, auditory to auditory and kinesthetic to kinesthetic you are speaking the same language as the other person, and you are building rapport. This technique is very powerful in developing mutual understanding and respect.

A R.E.A.L. Tip

SEE. HEAR. FEEL. What verbal cues are you getting? Listen closely to how people are expressing themselves, and you will unlock the keys to communicating more effectively with them.

I have provided you with tools to interview effectively so you can recruit the right people at the right time and in the right place. The next challenge is: Once you have the right people, how do you retain them? Let us look at what people seek from their employers.

What Employees Really Seek

The compensation trap catches many organizations: investing a lot of time and money in complex compensation structures and strategies, and not paying attention to what employees want most.

According to *Harvard Study* in 2009, these are the top priorities that employees want in their workplace:

- Feeling "in" on things.

- Appreciation for a job well done.

- Management support.

- Growth and development.

- Job security and wages.

- Honest, constructive feedback.

A retention program is not a silo that sits in human resources and consists of dress-down Fridays or pizza Thursdays. Instead, retention begins with the purpose, vision and values I talked about in chapter one. You cannot feel "in" on anything if you do not know what "it" is.

Your employees want to feel they are part of a larger purpose. We live in a world where the triple bottom-line of "People, Profit, Planet" has become part of a new conversation about the relationship between companies and the people they serve. That means your employees have high expectations of what they want you to stand for. They need to see how the company makes the world a better place, how their individual efforts make a difference and how their individual goals connect to the larger organizational goals.

Here is a team exercise to help your group gain consensus on what they believe are the most important factors contributing to employee morale.

Instructions

In the "Individual" column, have each manager/supervisor rank the factors from 1-10 based on what she, as an individual manager, believes is the most important factor contributing to employee morale in the organization/department. Use 1 to indicate the most important factor and 10 for the least important.

Once each manager has completed ranking the factors individually, have them discuss the rankings in groups of three-to-four individuals. Then, in the "Group" column have the groups agree on the ranking for each factor.

Team Exercise: What Do People Want From Their Jobs?

Individual	Group	Factors	Managers/ Supervisors	Employees
		Feeling of being "in" on things.		
		Full appreciation of work done.		
		Understanding of personal situations.		
		Good working conditions.		
		Promotion in the company.		
		High wages.		
		Tactful discipline.		
		Job security.		
		Personal loyalty of supervisor.		
		Interesting work.		

Various organizations do this study often. To compare your organization to the standards, see the chart, which highlights what managers/supervisors in these studies believe employees want from the organization compared to what employees seek from the organization. The results are very telling. The top-three rankings for managers/supervisors focus on wages, promotions and job security, while employees stated they want to feel appreciation for their work, feel "in" on things and have their managers/supervisors understand personal issues.

What Do People Want From Their Jobs?

Factors	Managers/ Supervisors	Employees
Feeling of being "in" on things.	10	2
Full appreciation of work done.	8	1
Understanding of personal situations.	9	3
Good working conditions.	4	9
Promotion in the company.	3	7
High wages.	1	5
Tactful discipline.	7	10
Job security.	2	4
Personal loyalty of supervisor.	6	8
Interesting work.	5	6

The message is very clear—to retain the high-quality people you hire, you need to show appreciation for work well done and help them feel valued for their efforts. The result? You will not only retain them, they also will be highly motivated to excel, be more engaged and offer creative and innovative solutions to business issues as part of a responsibility-based culture I discussed earlier.

You can see retention does not fit neatly into a single file. Instead, retention is about engaging and empowering employees, enriching their lives and providing a motivating work environment. I call it The Big E, and that is our next stop.

Chapter Four
The Big E Equals Increased Earnings

> *"Workers have three primary needs: interesting work,*
> *recognition for doing a good job, and being let in on things*
> *that are going on in the company."*
>
> —*Zig Ziglar*

In response to the brutal economic and workplace changes that occurred between 2008 and 2010, research by Gallup shows more than two-thirds of American workers are either not engaged in their workplaces—just putting in their time—or actively disengaged in their workplaces—unhappy and spreading their discontent.[xvii]

Hewitt Associates conducted another research study about employee engagement in 900 organizations. It showed decreases in engagement on the rise. Below are the statistics from 2009 to 2010.

	Increase in engagement	Decrease in engagement
Q2 2009	41%	28%
Q3 2009	38%	30%
Q4 2009	46%	31%
Q1 2010	31%	37%
Q2 2010	30%	46%

Note: Based on study of engagement in 900 organizations
Source: Hewitt Associates

And what is the cost of disengagement? Higher turnover rates. Weak leadership. Lack of ideas. When people are disengaged, creativity and innovation become nonexistent. Productivity suffers because people are not in problemsolving mode. They are watching the clock instead of coming up with new ways of doing things.

At the Society for Human Resource Management (SHRM) annual conference in June 2008, a leading research and consulting company, ISR, announced the results of a new global employee engagement study. Gathering surveys from over 660,000 employees from around the world, the data shows a dramatic difference in bottom-line results between companies with highly engaged employees and those with low levels of engagement.

The table below shows significant gaps in performance on net income growth and improvement in earnings per share (EPS) over a one-year period.

	Percentage Growth Operating Income	Percentage Growth Net Income	Percentage Improvement Earnings Per Share
Companies with **Low** Employee Engagement	-32.7	-3.8	-11.2
Companies with **High** Employee Engagement	+19.2	+13.2	+27.8

With these kinds of results. the importance of engagement is very apparent. So let us start. How do you engage employees in every economy?

It can seem overwhelming. That is why I break it down into seven steps, so my clients can clearly see how to make The Big E come alive in their organizations.

The Engagement and Empowerment Process for Improvement

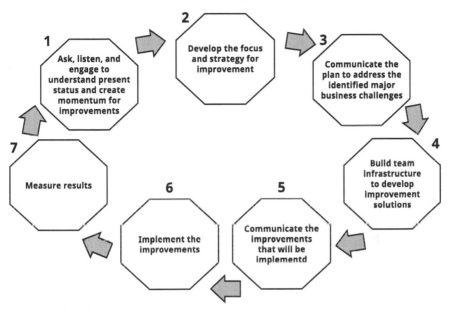

1. Ask, Listen and Engage

Avoid the dynamic of sending down the solution from on high. We have all been there when the "grown ups," aka, senior management, come back from a retreat and then spread the gospel to the "kids," aka, the employees. The message is that management is telling employees what to do instead of involving employees in the process.

When you ask and listen, you understand the current status, and then you can engage your employees in the process for improvement. How do you ask and listen?

Here are just a few ways to get the dialogue started:

- In-depth employee observation, not unlike traditional anthropological research.

- Employee focus groups.

- One-on-one employee interviews.

- Company task force.

- Companywide survey.

- Interviews with outside stakeholders and industry observers.

Dianne M. Durkin with Carey Earle

What to ask? Here are six key questions I think every company should ask its employees:

1. What is the present level of pride in and commitment to this organization?

2. What are the top three strengths of the organization?

3. What are the top three areas needing improvement within the organization?

4. What do you personally need to better contribute to the overall growth, profitability and customer satisfaction levels of the organization?

5. If you could give one message to senior management, what would it be?

6. What one thing would you recommend we should stop doing as a company?

I stated questions are the secret weapons of Magnetic Leadership. With this process, people feel listened to, they feel their input is valued, most importantly, it creates momentum for improvement. You will be amazed at the suggestions you receive, especially from the front line.

2. Develop the Focus and Strategy for Improvement

Now comes a critical step. It is great to listen; now it is time to take action on what you heard and learned. Compiling the information, categorizing it, analyzing it and putting a focused plan into action is imperative.

Prioritization is a key success factor. If you try to do everything, nothing will get done properly. Step 2 is all about laser-focusing on the key areas for improvement and developing a strategy to address them.

Throughout my work with hundreds of clients, I have found that in addition to operational enhancements, there are three things I hear them say in Step 1:

"What is our vision and strategy for the future?"

"Communications from the manager to employee and from department to department are far too poor."

"Appreciation is non-existent. We rarely receive positive feedback, and yet if something is wrong, we know it instantly."

Think about these comments in connection with the primary motivators for people in the work environment discussed in the last chapter:

People want to "feel in on things." They want a clear vision, purpose and strategy, and in order to ensure everyone understands it, it must be communicated in a clear, concise and consistent manner.

Appreciation. It was number one. It is the magic that helps people to be engaged and to improve operating performance.

The message to senior management is obvious: clearly articulate your vision and strategy and help individuals understand how their work contributes to achieving both. Simplicity for understanding is key. Make sure your purpose and vision are simple and accessible and your employees can identify with it. A meaningful purpose can go a long way in connecting and motivating them.

See how the simplicity shines through in these two purpose statements from Ritz-Carlton and Disney.

Ritz-Carlton—*Ladies and gentlemen serving ladies and gentlemen.*

Disney—*To use our imagination to bring happiness to millions.*

If you engage your employees in developing the purpose, vision and values, and creating the future, you have the foundation for improvement and growth.

Remember in chapter one when we discussed the mission of an N.Y.-based HMO and the values described in the Swedwood Way of Life? Both were developed by the employees. This engagement process led to the development of a foundation of trust.

I talked earlier about values. Your strategy for improvement must incorporate your values. It has to ring true as an authentic part of making your company the best that it can be at its very core. You then have to share the vision and values with the same people who helped you shape it: your employees. That is what leads us to Step 3.

Look at this graphic from an employee's perspective. In order for your team to engage in the bold steps it will take to fulfill your goals, they have to buy into and support your vision and purpose. You need to make sure they understand where the company is going and what their role is in getting the company there.

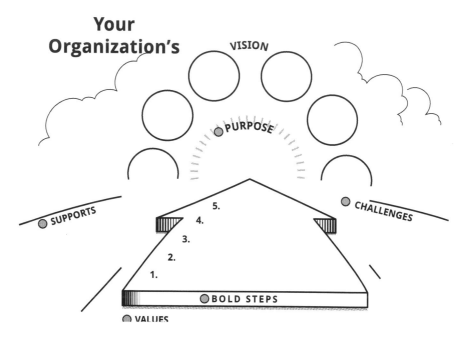

Source: Grove Consultants International.

A R.E.A.L. Tip

If employees do not know where you are going and what their role is in getting you there, why do they care?

3. Communicate the Plan to Address the Identified Major Business Improvements

Many organizations spend a lot of time creating complex communication strategies. Instead of going down that path, think of ways to paint the full picture for your employees. Remember, 60 percent of the population is visual—paint a picture!

Communication only works when your managers and employees are communicating with each other. Communicating is a two way street. Let us look at some communication techniques that have communication operating at a higher level in your organization.

Communicate in context

When you communicate to your employees, make sure you are looking at the communication from their perspective. Be sure to answer the subliminal question in employees' minds, "What is in it for me?" For example, if I am a line worker at a manufacturing facility, I want to know how change impacts me. How many more people are we adding? Will I have to work more overtime? Do I need additional training?

Forums of understanding

Make sure people receive communication in the way you intend it to be. Remember, it is not enough to push the message out – people need to understand it. For example, if people are feeling uneasy about change, there needs to be a forum or a conduit for them to express their concerns and then a time and place to address those concerns. Real connection comes from both expression and actions that say loudly: "They heard me!"

Sustaining communication

How do you know when your communication plan takes flight? It is when people begin trading stories and ideas. That is when you know they are "internalizing the message." This can happen in focus groups, work teams or individual conversations. When the communication grows organically, it becomes a participative plan that is sustainable in your organization

A R.E.A.L. Tip

When developing your communication, follow the Native American adage and "Walk a mile in their moccasins."

4.   Build Team Infrastructure to Develop Business Solutions

When you build your team infrastructure around the major business issues identified by the employees in step one, your employee engagement and empowerment become the stars of the show. Consider setting up cross-functional teams of six-to-eight individuals to solve the major business issue. By having a cross-functional group, you bring different skill sets to the table. The result? You have a better chance of addressing the issues more successfully.

Here is an invaluable chart. It provides the team with the full picture of what they need to consider in developing the total solution. Remember, 60 percent of the population is visual – this shows them the entire process and illustrates everything they need to consider to solve the business issue.

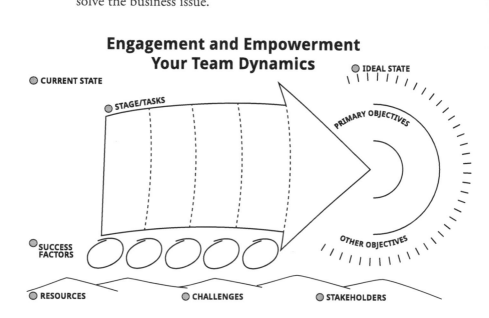

Source: Grove Consultants International

Let us define the components from the chart above.

- **Current State:** This is where the organization is today on this issue. At this stage, the team gathers both quantitative and qualitative information on the existing situation.

- **Ideal State:** This is where the group feels it would like to be – and answers the question: what is ideal for growth?

- **Stages/Tasks:** In this phase, the teams document the step-by-step process to achieve the ideal state.

- **Success Factors:** In order to achieve the ideal state, these are the factors critical to success. The team identifies what has to happen to reach the ideal state.

- **Resources:** This identifies the resources needed to reach the ideal stated goal.

- **Challenges:** These are the barriers to success. The team suggests how to remove these.

- **Stakeholders:** Here are the people needed to engage in this process. When the team completes this chart, senior management can clearly see the entire picture and process. When people see it, then they can believe it!

Clearly define team roles and responsibilities

Putting a group of people together with cross skills and calling them a "team" is just the beginning. If they have never worked together before, they need guidance and direction on everything from non-performing and disruptive team members to conflicting objectives.

This often takes an experienced facilitator who can address the various personalities and focus the group, handle hidden agendas and ask the tough questions. We throw the word "team" around a lot, so I think it is good to remind people of its definition.

A T.E.A.M. brings out the best in everyone because:

Together Everyone Achieves More

Sounds corny, but it is true. Ask anyone who has been on a high-performing team, and they will nod knowingly.

5. Communicate the Improvements that Will Be Implemented

You have heard me say several times, you cannot over communicate. With all the information overload in our lives, it takes a lot of communication for us to break through to our employees. Have you heard the communication adage: "Tell them, tell them what you told them, then tell them again?"

When it comes to communicating during any kind of change, those words ring true. Keep a consistent flow of communication, and people feel they are "in the know." I have seen many times that the ongoing evidence of their company's commitment to their satisfaction, career growth and personal development energizes employees.

It is critical to understand that communication is not something you complete by checking it off the list. Instead, you need to foster ongoing success through continuous evaluation and feedback. This is where the coaching techniques that I discuss later in this chapter come in handy.

6. Implement the Improvements

Nothing changes attitudes faster than when people see words take action. To hear: "This is the plan," then to see their role in it and finally to see it live and in motion. That is powerful because it shows movement and tenacity, important parts of Magnetic Leadership. The opposite is also true. If you announce plans and follow it with a deafening silence and no action, it is a clear message that nothing is happening. It is one of those things that make employees cynical because it happens so often. Break that notion, and show some motion!

7. Measure Results

A good friend of mine in the project management business lives by the mantra: "What gets measured gets done." And I could not agree more. Measuring is a commitment to look at what is working and what is not and puts your organization on a track of continuous improvement. Whatever the business issue, make sure you have identified the key measurement criteria that are appropriate for your industry. In addition to standard business measurements such as return on equity or growth in earnings per share, many companies also want to measure employee satisfaction, customer satisfaction and brand recognition. Let us take a quick look at these.

Employee satisfaction

Annual checkups measure employee satisfaction, and they can take the form of one-on-one interviews with key employees, cross-functional focus groups or company-wide surveys. Paying attention to retention statistics can provide valuable insights. My belief is you must have a balance of both qualitative and quantitative information so you capture the data and the emotional pulse of the organization.

Customer satisfaction

Increased sales, repeat clients and referrals are all good indicators, but you need to make sure you are also capturing "the voice of the customer." For example, look at all the places in your business pipeline where someone actually speaks to the customer. Whether it is a customer service agent on the phone or in an online chat, you need to make sure you capture customer feedback that points to strengths and weaknesses. Many companies see social media platforms like Twitter and Facebook as a way to hear what customers are saying in real time.

Brand recognition

Engaged and empowered employees take good care of customers and nurture strong relationships with your brand. When your customers trust that your brand will fulfill its promise of quality, service and satisfaction again and again, you no longer have to compete on price. Brand recognition and brand loyalty are key differentiators in any market place. When customers can clearly tell you how you are different and why they choose you over the competition, you have achieved brand loyalty.

These are three examples of areas where you can focus and measure. However, make sure you are measuring what matters to you. If employee retention is your focus, make sure you are measuring employee satisfaction.

There is a reason they use the big thermometer for fundraising efforts. It shows progress and lets everyone see where they are in the process. Figure out what you are measuring, and then find your company's version of the big thermometer to show it.

Now, when you look at all the elements for Engagement and Empowerment, there is a common factor. Each step requires people. Without people, nothing is going to happen. In the previous chapter, I talked about how to recruit the right people at the right time and in the right place. Now let us look at additional ways to develop those people to engage and empower them at every stage of the game.

Provide development opportunities

Think about how you handle employee development. Nothing is more engaging than a person striving to achieve a future goal and knowing they have the confidence and support of management.

Go for it

A stretch assignment can be highly motivating for an employee because it communicates your belief that the employee has the ability to reach beyond what she is doing right now. It is the next step beyond those important words: "Good job!" It says, "We believe in you, and you have the talent to take on a challenge." It tells the employee to "Go for it!"

Coaching Instead of Coaxing

Many organizations promote (or sometimes push) individuals into roles before they are ready. There is a difference between challenging employees and pushing them out of the nest when they are not ready to fly. Coaching gives them the security of a parachute. Everyone at every level needs a parachute— from the CEO to the janitor. Everyone needs a good manager to coach and develop them. Today, more than ever, CEOs need to have that outside counsel to help them strategize about how to deal with the complex, changing business climate of running an organization. It can get very lonely at the top.

What is coaching? Is it telling people what to do? No!

Coaching is asking, not telling. It is recognizing that the answers lie within the person. At its best, coaching helps employees come up with a solution rather than providing one for them. It is teaching them to fish rather than giving them the fish. The ultimate desired outcome of coaching is motivating employees to use their expertise and talents to be the best they can be.

Three results of good coaching
1. **Improved employee development in an organization.**
2. **Individual improvement that not only increases confidence, but also builds a stronger connection to the organization.**
3. **Increased self-awareness allowing individuals to recognize their own developmental areas.**

From mentoring and managing expectations to conducting performance reviews or reaching team objectives, coaching can take many forms. Regardless of the form it takes, the objective is the same—*to positively motivate the individual.*

When I talk about motivation, I am not referring to the stereotypical content of self-help tapes and books. Magnetic Leaders use intrinsic motivation as a key tool when they coach. Intrinsic motivation comes from the inside of an individual versus an outside reward or expectation. It comes from the pure pleasure associated with a job well-done. A Magnetic Leader cultivates intrinsic motivation by:

- Providing a vision of optimism and hope.

- Creating a positive, constructive work environment.

- Encouraging individuals to take responsibility for their actions.

- Developing a habit of continual "positive thought" in employees.

- Allowing employees to improve through positive encouragement.

When I am training leaders to be better coaches, I find that following this five-step process provides a simple and systematic road map.

Five-step Coaching Process

1. **Gain agreement that there is an area for improvement or development.**

    - Ask questions to develop the issue and get more information.

    - Use checkpoint summaries to organize the issues and actions.

    - End with a question to gain agreement.

2. **Discuss alternative options for managing or solving the situation.**

    - Ask questions to clearly identify options to address this issue.

    - Use checkpoint summaries to organize the issues and actions.

    - End with a question to gain agreement.

3. **Agree on action to manage or solve the situation.**

    - Ask questions to identify an action plan.

    - Use checkpoint summaries to organize the issues and actions.

    - Restate the action steps, set a time frame for follow-up and end with a question to gain agreement.

4. **Follow up to ensure the person is acting in accordance with the agreement.**

   - Recap the agreed-upon action plan.

   - Ask questions to determine the progress to date.

   - Outline the progress to date and next steps as you understand them.

   - Restate next steps, and ask a question to gain agreement.

5. **Reinforce any achievement or performance improvement.**

   - Praise them for any progress they have made.

   - Provide constructive feedback on areas still needing improvement.

   - Recognize performance, reward results.

You may notice questions are the first item in each of the steps. Questions are truly the "secret weapon" in coaching. With an effective questioning strategy, people can develop their own solutions and are then more motivated to implement the actions. After all, they developed their own solution; it is not someone else telling them what to do or not do. Let us look at some preparation and key questions to ask.

Preparation and Key Questions to Ask When Planning a Coaching Discussion

Before you begin a coaching discussion, make sure you are prepared with the information you need to make the discussion productive and positive. In preparation, ask yourself the following questions:

- What is the performance issue or development opportunity this employee needs to work on?

- What are the motivational needs of this person?

- How can I challenge this person to master the elements of his job?

- Does this person have some fears or concerns he may be expressing? If so, what are they?

- What is the ideal result after the discussion?

These questions help prepare you to deal with various aspects of the complexities that may exist with each person. Preparation is key. Being unprepared can send the worst possible messages, such as:

- You are not important.

- You are not valued.

Do not underestimate the power of preparation. It is now time to look at some step-by-step questions, remembering that the objective is to have the person develop his own solutions. As with interviewing, open-ended questions and high-impact questions are magic. Be sure to allow for open discussions and creativity. Below are some sample questions and checkpoint summaries for each step of the process.

Step 1: Gain agreement

Ask questions to define the issues or development area:

- In your estimation, how are things going?

- Are you getting the results you want?

Use a checkpoint questioning approach to organize the issues and gain agreement that there is a performance issue or a specific development need. Summarize what you heard:

- If I hear you correctly, you are not getting the results you want in _____?

- Do you agree this is the primary area we should work on over the next _____?

Step 2: Discuss options

As you work with the individual to brainstorm options, it is imperative you determine what is influencing performance. You want as many options or ideas as possible to come from the person being coached. Ask questions to clearly identify options to address this issue:

- What steps should we take to address this issue?

- In order to improve in this area, do you need to learn something new or practice doing something in another manner?

Use a checkpoint questioning approach to organize the issues, gain agreement and summarize what you have heard:

- If I understand your comments, you think the following options may help resolve the situation _____?

- Do you agree we should proceed by addressing this option and try to resolve this situation?

Step 3: Agree on actions

Ask questions to identify an action plan:

- What specific things should you and I do?

Use a checkpoint questioning approach to organize the issues and actions. Re-state the action steps, set a time frame for follow up and end with a question to gain agreement:

- I am going to do the following _____, and you are going to do the following _____. Let us check in on _____. Does this make sense to you?

A R.E.A.L. Tip

Repeat key words and phrases when you are coaching, so people feel heard when they hear their own thoughts reflected back to them.

Step 4: Follow up

Ask questions to determine the progress to date:

- We agreed we were going to work on the following _____.

- How has it been going?

- Do we need to make any adjustments to our plan?

Restate next steps, and ask a question to gain agreement:

- Based upon our progress thus far, I suggest we _____.

- Does this make sense to you?

Step 5: Reinforcement

Praise them for any progress they have made.

Ask questions to reinforce the behavior:

- How do you feel about what you have been able to achieve?

- Did this process work effectively for you?

Use checkpoint summaries to recognize positive actions:

- You have made great progress. Let us determine how I can support you in other areas you would like to improve upon.

Now, let us look at another critical element of coaching—feedback.

The Power of Feedback

You should view feedback as a valuable gift to another person. It is a potent communication skill. When we direct it to others, we can build them up or tear them down. By using feedback to support and empower other people, we build trust and enhance our relationship with them. Feedback offers three paramount functions in the development process:

1. **Feedback reinforces** - Positive reinforcement (think: "Great job - keep it up!") gives people a feeling of satisfaction with their performance. More importantly, it instills a desire to repeat the performance. It is like a treat for humans, a verbal biscuit that makes us want to do it again!

2. **Feedback informs** - Specific information regarding execution is crucial to both the current performance and task repeatability. If it is vague, it is not helpful.

3. **Feedback motivates** - Feedback, when initiated in a constructive manner, provides incentive and motivates employees to achieve higher performance levels.

It is important that you give feedback in a way that develops a connection instead of cutting off communication. To do this, feedback should be supportive:

- Supportive feedback is clear, immediate and non-judgmental, and it invites a positive response from the person who receives it.

- Non-supportive feedback is accusatory and judgmental, sometimes even obscure, and puts the other person off.

To be effective, feedback needs to be:

- **Constructive**—comes from the positive, providing suggestions for improvements rather than just criticism of current behavior.

- **Clear**—precise, meaningful and provides useful information in an easy-to-understand format.

- **Concise**—specific and free from superfluous detail. When you provide too much information, the intended message can get lost.

- **Consistent**—free from contradiction.

- **Timely**—comes as soon as appropriate after the behavior—and is not clouded by ensuing events.

A R.E.A.L. Tip

Let coaching be the parachute for employees as they jump into new opportunities.

Coaching is one way to make your employees feel they matter. Taking it a step further, we will look at employee enrichment and how you can support the whole life of your employees.

Employee Enrichment

Employee enrichment looks at the complete life of employees—not just their work lives.

- It takes a holistic approach that goes beyond work-life balance.

- It is what I call the Balanced Wheel of Success.

Even for the most successful people, life can sometimes feel overwhelming. The Balanced Wheel of Success helps us take a deep breath and look at our lives from every perspective. In my work inside of companies, I find this tool to be very calming and inspiring for employees at every level of the organization.

In the center of the wheel are Vision and Values. This encourages employees to think about where they are going and what their own guiding principles are.

I identify eight areas of focus in the Balanced Wheel of Success. These are a good place to start, and you can alter them to reflect individual needs:

- Financial.
- Physical.
- Intellectual/emotional.
- Social.
- Family.
- Professional/career.
- Friendship/relationship.
- Spiritual.

Mind-the-Gap Exercise

A good exercise when beginning work with The Balanced Wheel of Success is to ask employees what percentage of their time they currently spend in each area. Once they have that number, they should look again at each area and ask, "What percentage would I like to spend in each area?" If there is a gap between those two percentages, they should determine how they can close the gap between where they are today and where they want to be. This exercise is often both insightful and empowering because people get to take the time to think about these areas and realize they can make changes to align their time for a fuller, more meaningful life.

Just by having this discussion, employees know you care, and with that caring comes loyalty, engagement, creativity, innovation, responsibility, accountability and trust – all elements of a solid culture built on Magnetic Leadership. When people are happy, feel cared for and have a clear sense of their own vision, purpose and values, it is much easier for them to identify with and support the vision and similar values of the organization.

Key Areas to Consider

- **Financial:** what are your financial goals? Where are you today in terms of those goals? What changes or actions do you need to make to accomplish your goals?

- **Physical:** what are your health and fitness goals or challenges? What aspects of your health are you neglecting? What one change in your health would have the most impact on your well being? What keeps you from taking care of yourself? How can you remove those barriers?

- **Intellectual/emotional:** what challenges you intellectually? Do you have intellectual pursuits you have dropped along the way? Do you ever learn for the pure sake of learning versus learning to meet a goal? How is your emotional well being? Are there emotional issues standing in the way of your happiness?

- **Social:** what do you do when you are "at play?" One of the best stress relievers is having fun. What do you do to have fun? How do you spend time socially? Do you spend as much time as you would like with friends or family?

- **Family:** how much time do you have with your family? What is the quality of that time? Do you have time together when you are "at play" as a family? If someone asked your family how you spend the majority of your time, what would they say?

- **Professional/career:** how would you describe the trajectory of your career to date? What have you achieved? What would you like to achieve? Are you on the career path or journey you want to be on? If not, how can you change directions?

- **Friendship/relationship:** what role do friendships or relationships play in your life? Do people consider you a good friend? Do you think your friends would say you are there for them when they need you?

- **Spiritual:** do you have a spiritual life? Is there quiet time that is about pure reflection? Can you find joy in the everyday moments?

The Balanced Wheel of Success helps people to think about their life in a simple, yet systematic, way. It breaks down some of life's very big questions, and it is important to remember that balance is not perfection in each area;

rather it is the ongoing dance between them. If you spend all of your time dancing with finance, spiritual is a sad and wilted wallflower. Just as if you are dancing more with your career than your family, you can find yourself alone when you need the support of the people who love you. The purpose of the wheel is to provide insight and pathways for positive change.

Another powerful tool that helps in the enrichment process of your employees is a Life Vision Matrix. It helps people reflect on where they have been and where they want to go.

Here are 10 questions as part of the Life Vision Matrix exercise

1. **What in your lifetime are you most proud of having done?**

   _____

   _____

   _____

2. **What are the top three things you have achieved in your life?**

   _____

   _____

   _____

3. **What have you learned from your achievements?**

   _____

   _____

   _____

4. **What are the top three things you still want to achieve in your life?**

   _____

   _____

   _____

Dianne M. Durkin with Carey Earle

5. **What do you believe to be your major strengths?**

   _____

   _____

   _____

6. **What are your areas for development?**

   _____

   _____

   _____

7. **What types of things keep you up at night?**

   _____

   _____

   _____

8. **What motivates you?**

   _____

   _____

   _____

9. **How will you know if you are successful? Will you feel different? Do different things?**

   _____

   _____

   _____

10. **What would you like to achieve in your lifetime?**

   _____

   _____

   _____

Once you have answered the questions, use the chart below to look at your Life Vision in another powerful way.

Life Vision Matrix Exercise

Fill in your own experiences, interests and achievements in 10-year increments. For periods beyond your current age, record your goals for that period of your life.

Time frame	Experiences	Interests	Achievements
Age 1–10			
Age 11–20			
Age 21–30			
Age 31–40			
Age 41–50			

Time frame	Experiences	Interests	Achievements
Age 51–60			
Age 61–70			
Age 71–80			
Age 81–90			
Age 91–100			

The Life Vision Matrix is another way of setting life goals. The combination of the Balanced Wheel of Success, answering the 10 Life Vision Matrix questions and filling out the table provides people with a success plan for life.

A R.E.A.L. Tip

Magnetic Leadership looks at the whole person beginning with you and extending to everyone in your organization. It is enriching the lives of every employee. It is caring.

Creating an Environment for Success

With The Big E, I discussed employee engagement, empowerment and enrichment. We have one last stop, and that is the entire employee environment.

How do you create an environment where people feel cared for and ultimately perform at their very best?

The Edgewood Centre, a long-term care facility in Portsmouth, N.H., offers on-site daycare for its employees and then takes it a step further with intergenerational programming. For example, they bring their elderly residents together with the children in the onsite daycare center for entertainment or arts and crafts. It creates an environment of joy and life, bringing the old and young together. For the mothers who work there, they value getting to spend time with their children at lunch or during a group activity. It takes the pressure and stress off of the employees since they know their children are on-site and in good hands.

Create an environment that encourages creativity and inspiration, and/or offers a place to take a deep breath and regroup before jumping back into deadlines, discussions and distractions.

Blogger and Chief Happiness Officer Alexander Kjerful offers suggestions on "how to pimp your office." While this might not work in every culture, his ideas help you think outside the cubicle. Here are just a few of his ideas:

- An inviting bean-bag chair (great for impromptu brainstorming sessions).

- Desks made of unusual materials (such as the wing of DC3 plane).

- A bibliochiase—a chair designed to hold books and reference materials.

- A Stokke Garden—a chair that looks like a sculpture.

- A Conference Bike—where seven people pedal at once.

- Art tables—tables in cool and interesting designs and shapes.

Source: http://positivesharing.com/2007/03/12-ways-to-pimp-your-office/

The physical environment is just one part of the puzzle. Some of the more creative ideas presented above may not work in your culture. The important thing to remember is that with Magnetic Leadership, you need to consider the total environment—from benefits to management coaching to establishing vision, values and positioning. It is really everything you build around that environment. People often ask me, "Where do benefits fit in?" Below is a top-line look at some of the benefits packages of companies on Fortune's list of top companies to work for.

Consider SAS, the world's largest privately owned software company, where turnover is the industry's lowest at 10 percent.

Snapshot of benefits:[xviii]

- High-quality child care at $410 a month.

- Ninety-percent coverage of the health insurance premium.

- Unlimited sick days.

- A medical center staffed by four physicians.

- Ten nurse practitioners (at no cost to employees).

- A free 66,000-square-foot fitness center and natatorium.

- A lending library and a summer camp for children.

In a tough economy, another company, Google, increased employees' 401k matching program and gave them a stock-option exchange program to help them with underwater stock options. Another plus is engineers get to devote 20 percent of their time to projects they want to work on.

Here are some of their other benefits:

- Onsite childcare.

- Onsite fitness center.

- Subsidized gym memberships.

- Job-sharing program.

- Telecommuting.

- Domestic-partner benefits for same-sex couples

Wireless pioneer, Qualcomm, offers stock options upon hire and has a culture that includes an onsite farmer's market, baseball games, surfing lessons, kayaking tours, white-water rafting, bonfires and bowling.

Here are some of their other benefits:

- Healthcare coverage at 100 percent.

- Onsite fitness center.

- Subsidized gym membership.

- Job-sharing program.

- Compressed work week.

- Telecommuting.

- Domestic-partner benefits.

In the "churn and burn" world of management consulting, Boston Consulting group stands out with these benefits:

- Paid sabbaticals.

- Healthcare coverage at 100 percent.

- Job-sharing program.

- Compressed work week.

- Telecommuting.

- Domestic-partner benefits.

When Amazon acquired Zappos, CEO Tony Hsieh held a company meeting telling employees they would each receive a Kindle and a retention bonus equal to 40 percent of their annual salary.

Here are some of Zappos benefits:

- Healthcare coverage at 100 percent.

- Compressed work week.

- Domestic-partner benefits.

What stands out with these companies and their benefits is they are thinking about the whole life of the employee. In today's world, Blackberries® and iPhones® tether employees to their work, and there is a blurring of the lines between work life and personal life. The opportunity for Magnetic Leadership is to recognize this shift and place employees' personal and professional goals on the same level.

In this chapter, we engaged employees in discussions of both the strengths and areas for development in the company. We empowered them to use their creative thinking to help solve major business issues within a team structure. We also looked at ways to enrich your employees' lives—from the work environment to their own personal goals and ambitions. Now let us take a look at the letter "A" in Getting R.E.A.L.—the power of appreciation.

Chapter Five
Appreciation Creates Amazement

*"Appreciate everything your associates do for the business.
Nothing else can quite substitute for a few
well-chosen, well-timed and sincere words of praise.
They're absolutely free and worth a fortune."*

—**Sam Walton**

Once you have engaged, empowered and enriched employees' lives, you have their attention. To have their heart, they need to feel appreciated, rewarded, recognized and valued.

In its Employee Engagement Survey[xix] of 42,000 participants, Gallup estimated U.S. companies lose as much as $350 billion each year due to disengaged employees. Businesses, either in good or bad times, cannot afford these losses. Instead, they need to develop strategies to help employees feel valued. While they realize using incentives, especially recognition, is an effective method to ensure employees feel valued, many managers think money is the ultimate reward. It is important to remember rewards and recognition take many forms.

The June 2002 McKinsey Quality Survey showed "praise from immediate managers" and "leadership attention" are more powerful motivators than cash bonuses, raises and stock options. In difficult times when workloads are higher and the pressures are more intense, positive words of encouragement can be exactly what employees need.

The Hay Group says as many as 59 percent of the employees they surveyed are thinking about or seeking a new job. And you know your competitors will first recruit the best employees, the ones with the knowledge base and skill sets for the future growth of your organization.

To maintain your skilled workforce and your loyal and engaged employees, it is critical to make sure your employees know their efforts matter. Appreciation comes in all forms, shapes and sizes. The best meet the specific needs of the individual. Sometimes a $5 gift certificate to Starbucks, Dunkin Donuts or McDonalds—or a simple chocolate bar—can put a huge smile on someone's face and energize them with more than just a sugar high. It is amazing to see people light up. It is the simple things that make a difference. The simplest and most inexpensive are often words.

The Power of Words

"Thank you!" I often say these are the two most under-utilized words in the English language. When said with true sincerity, they are the most powerful words anyone can hear.

"Great Job!"

"I really appreciate all your work!"

These simple words mean a lot because we do not get to hear them often enough. Think of the small things that can make your day or even week. Usually, it is a gesture from someone acknowledging something you have done. Small things do matter. If you do not believe it, just get into the habit of thanking people and see what happens.

Growth opportunities

What is a bigger compliment than offering an opportunity or a challenge? Sometimes rewards and recognition take the form of a "stretch assignment" or a special project that is highly visibile within the organization.

When someone excels, they can share that knowledge. When a manager asks an employee to coach or mentor a colleague, it is a public recognition of that person's talent and skill.

Training and development is highly valued by many employees because it is an investment in their skills and their future. It tells them, "you are important to us, and we want to invest in you."

Spotlight on sabbaticals

Some organizations offer sabbaticals where an employee can take a long period of time off. Sixteen percent of American companies offer unpaid sabbaticals and another 5 percent offer paid sabbaticals, according to SHRM.

The web site www.yoursabbatical.com defines sabbaticals as:

"…planned, strategic job pauses that allow you to travel, do research, volunteer, learn a new skill, or fulfill a lifelong dream. The most meaningful sabbaticals are planned ones – with specific goals and objectives designed to benefit you and your company."

What types of sabbaticals are there? Here are the different kinds of sabbaticals identified on www.yoursabbatical.com:

Travel Sabbatical

See the world or just be part of it. Experiencing another culture never fails to provide a new perspective on what individuals have at home.

Green Sabbatical

Tap into social responsibility and give employees time out to help with a clean-up project, further a renewable energy effort or do field research.

Volunteer Sabbatical

This program gives employees an opportunity to donate time to a charity they and their companies believe in, such as Habitat for Humanity, teaching English to Guatemalan children or helping with a church missionary project. The possibilities are endless and endlessly rewarding.

Innovation Sabbatical

This program stimulates fresh thinking by giving employees the opportunity to experience a different work culture, inside or outside their own industry. Upon their return, the insight they gained while "out of the box" fuels their creative juices and provides fresh inspiration for their coworkers as well.

Family Sabbatical

Many companies give employees the opportunity to spend time with their children or take a trip with an aging parent. Providing a solid block of quality time with family members helps these people balance their priorities and gain perspective and renewed energy for their workplace objectives.

Learning Sabbatical

Educational sabbaticals enable employees to finish an MBA, become fluent in a second language and earn certification in a software program and more.

Research Sabbatical

These programs enable employees to take time out to develop a new product or business process, or work on a project, book or theory.

Lifelong Goal Sabbatical

This program allows employees to re-energize themselves by chasing a lifelong dream such as acting in a theater production, competing in a triathlon or hiking Mt. Everest. Going after an audacious goal – and conquering it – can create powerful momentum for the individual and the company that fosters that achievement.

Personal Growth Sabbatical

This time out for self-reflection can take the form of a silent meditation retreat, reading a stack of self-help books or even filling up a journal with reflections, hopes and plans. Regardless of which one they choose, individuals return with a personal clarity that might not have been possible otherwise.

Hybrid Sabbatical

This program allows employees to plan a sabbatical that includes two or more of the above.

Source: www.yoursabbatical.com

Another growth opportunity in today's global business culture is the opportunity to learn a language. Providing language training and incentives can be a powerful retention tool and can go a long way to making an employee feel appreciated and recognized.

Woody Allen famously said: "Eighty percent of success is showing up." When it comes to recognition, consider giving employees the opportunity to show up in a special spotlight. Invite them to an important senior-level meeting. Ask them to present their idea at a team meeting. Let them shine and feel the energy of recognition! Here are some examples of specific tributes you can offer:

Tributes

Think about what is valued in your organization. Is it a technology gadget like the iPad® or a gift certificate to a renowned restaurant? Here are some ideas to get you started:

- Time off or comp time.

- Movie tickets.

- Travel tickets.

- Health-club memberships.

- Theater tickets.

To be effective, all rewards and recognition must be:

- **Timely:** Recognition should be as immediate as possible. If you do not thank someone until long after the effort, it diminishes the importance and sincerity.

- **Continual:** Do not be haphazard, making rewards seem like afterthoughts. It should be an ongoing part of your culture.

- **Customized:** Rewards and recognition need to make sense in your culture and to your employees.

- **Balanced:** Think about appropriate levels of gratitude for the action you are recognizing. For example, offering a gift certificate to say thank you for a job well done and something more substantial when someone has achieved a milestone for the organization.

Frank Mulhern, the academic director for the Forum for People Performance Management and Measurement at Northwestern University, offers these tips:

- **Think of your employees as customers** and segment them according to their needs and their lives. Remember, a single 20-something is different from a married 40-something with a family living in the suburbs.

- **Understand what matters to your employees.** Ask them and survey them, and act upon their feedback.

- **Make sure human resources is not just the legal department for people issues.** There should be a component of nurturing and fostering employee experiences.

- **Develop an overarching employee strategy** that encompasses recognition, retention, communication and benefits.

- **Create an environment where employees can interact.** Good relationships at work are an important part of employee satisfaction.

Source: Return on Performance. 2010 Spring Issue. People-First Leadership by Leslie Vryenhoek.

Snapshots of Rewards and Recognition

Would you like to see your CEO pushing the coffee cart, or would you like to have meetings while walking? Here are some snapshots of rewards and recognition to ignite your creativity.

Passing the buck in a positive way

AdvancedMD CEO, Jim Pack, handwrites thank-you notes to employees on a $2 bill.

Celebrating innovative thinking

Calgon created an annual award for the "best idea that didn't work," which is presented at the annual awards dinner to stimulate innovation over winning.

Cream or sugar?

During the busiest times of the year, Cigna Group executives push coffee carts around the office serving drinks and refreshments to their colleagues.

Birthday breakfast

Cisco System's CEO, John Chambers, hosts a monthly hour-long birthday breakfast for any employee with a birthday that month.

Walk and talk

The City of Dallas sponsored a walkathon where employees set goals for walking a certain number of steps each day, offering a free gym membership to those who walked the farthest. Beyond working out, their walks became traveling staff meetings. After the program ended, teams still continued the walk–and-talk staff meetings.

Source: HR World, 25 Ways to Reward Employees (Without Spending a Dime) By Dan Tynan www.hrworld.com

Creating rock stars

"A Supervisor within our building distributes rocks as awards. The rocks can range in size from a tennis ball to a football, and each is hand-painted with "YOU ROCK!" or "You're a ROCKSTAR!" Along with being free and very well received by the recipients, they also serve as a great conversation piece sitting on a desk and have encouraged other colleagues to adapt similar ideas, thereby increasing the level of overall recognition." Jeff, U.S. Bank

Words to treasure

"I have a note that my director wrote from 10 years ago. It always makes me feel good to go back and read it when work is getting me down. Last month I gave each of my 98 employees a wooden box with a letter inside encouraging them to use the box as a treasure box—a treasure of kind words, thank you cards, words of encouragement or recognition so that they too could go back and read them." —Kathy, Forrest General Hospital

Source: www.maketheirday.com

As you can see from the examples, small gestures can go a long way. Are you ready to ask your employees for some ideas? Here is a brainstorming exercise that can help you uncover some hidden gems in your organization.

Rev up the Energy with a Recognition and Reward Brainstorm

One way to make sure your reward and recognition programs hit the mark is to ask for input when creating them. Depending upon the size of your organization, create teams and assign them to brainstorm ideas to reward themselves. Ask them to answer these questions:

- What motivates people to grow?
- What inspires people to innovate?
- What encourages people to take risks?
- What makes people feel valued?

- What makes people proud?

- What makes people shine?

Ask them to brainstorm ideas at three levels:

1. **Thank you**—most basic form of recognition.
2. **Growth opportunities**—from training to stretch assignments.
3. **Specific tributes**—from tickets to an event to a travel reward.

Once you review all the ideas, recognize people's contributions and select the best ideas to implement.

You can also use the book "1001 Ways to Reward Employees," by Bob Nelson to help give your teams ideas.

A R.E.A.L. Tip

Use these three ways to recognize people:

1. Simple thank yous.
2. Growth opportunities and stretch assignments.
3. Specific tributes like theatre or sports tickets.

Reflecting on Your Role as a Leader

As a leader, you need to be aware of how you recognize people and also how you receive ideas. When it comes to recognition, remember that giving people recognition is something everyone in an organization can do. As a leader, it is up to you to model the behavior and empower your managers to do the same. Below is a quick assessment that reminds all of us of the recognition and receptivity guidelines we can use daily.

Recognition guidelines

- Consistently look for opportunities to "catch people doing things right" and acknowledge them.

- Give praise that is genuine and appropriate.

Dianne M. Durkin with Carey Earle

- When you give praise, be sensitive to how other people may like to receive it.

- Say thank you when others praise you or encourage you.

Receptivity guidelines

Without creativity, organizations stagnate and eventually die. Being open to new ideas – no matter where they come from – is critical for an organization to remain competitive. As leaders you need to:

- Listen to new ideas without prematurely judging them because of what you already know, or who is putting the idea forward.

- Ask questions to make sure you understand what others are saying before making a decision about it.

- Be willing to listen to new ideas and create an environment where people are comfortable sharing more ideas in the future.

- Be receptive to feedback about your own performance and listen to it when it is given.

- Demonstrate a willingness to adapt the way you do things in response to other's suggestions.

As you read these guidelines, put a star next to what you are already doing well and an exclamation point by those you want to work on.

Now that you know rewards and recognition are not "one size fits all," let us take a look at it from a generational perspective.

A Magnetic Leaders Guide to Juggling the Generations

By 2011, the youngest Baby Boomers turn 65. So, the "boomer perspective," which has ruled for the last three decades, has to change in order to work with Generation X and Generation Y. From recruiting to rewarding, managers must avoid the temptation of looking at their employees as one mass group and instead, see them as individuals.

Generations X and Y have seen their parents and loved ones "downsized" and "right-sized." They have seen the pros and cons of an interdependent global economy. They watched Sept. 11 unfold on TV, and now they see global crises played out in real time on the Internet. They do not expect a company to take care of them for life. Instead, they expect to enjoy their lives. For them, work-life balance is not just a concept, it is an expectation.

Magnetic Leadership looks across the spectrum of generations to effectively communicate with people and connect with them. Let us start first with an overview of the top requirements of the younger generations, and then we can delve into each generation.

What are Generations X and Y looking for?

- A fun work environment.

- Growth opportunities and training and development programs.

- Understanding how the company's products create a better world.

- Wide range of projects to work on.

- A culture that values ideas, creativity and innovation.

- Assistance without micromanagement.

- Regular feedback and recognition.

- Teamwork and collaboration.

- High-quality management and leadership.

- Competitive salaries and good benefits (healthcare, profit sharing, 401K and tuition reimbursement)

- Balanced life.

The career goals of each generation are different.[xx] That is why the listening skills that I emphasized earlier are so important. A Baby Boomer cannot assume or judge what a Generation X or Generation Y employee or job candidate wants. You have to understand that each of these generations is looking at life differently, and the organizations that know how to harness the strengths of each generation will thrive.

Top-line Look at Career Goals of Each Generation

The Veterans (Born 1922-1943): Build a legacy.

Baby Boomers (Born 1943-1960): Build a stellar career.

Generation X (Born 1960-1980): Build a portable career.

Generation Y/Millennials (Born 1980-2000): Build parallel careers.

Beginning with the Veterans, let us drill down into each generation. Below are summary charts for each generation.

The Veterans 1922-1943

"Even though I am able to use the Internet fairly comfortably, the speed at which technology changes is sometimes overwhelming. Could I learn it if I want to? I really think I could. For me a lot of my lack of enthusiasm for all these gadgets is due to lack of interest. I have a cell phone, but have never had a reason to text message or play games on it. I use it to call people. I don't usually care for television programs in the first place enough to record them via TiVo or whatever recording devise the cable company wants to sell you. I like to read, garden and visit with friends and family."—A member of the Veteran generation posting to www.generationworkplace.com

Values	Assets	Liabilities
• Civic pride. • Loyalty. • Respect for authority. • Dedication/sacrifice. • Conformity. • Delayed reward. • Duty before pleasure. • Adherence to rules. • Honor. • Discipline.	• Stable. • Detail oriented. • Thorough. • Loyal. • Hard working.	• Inept with ambiguity. • Reluctant to buck the system. • Uncomfortable with conflict. • Reticent when they disagree.

Business Traits	View of Work	Working on Teams
• Directive leadership style that people may view as overbearing. • Tend to buck the authority of younger managers. • Can get stuck in "we have never done it that way". • Technology can be confusing and intimidating.	• Work is a privilege – they are grateful to have it. • Willing to work hard to get things accomplished. They are loyal, dependable and persistent. • Confident in own abilities. Taught to respect leaders and their institutions. • Believe hard work and sacrifice will pay off over the long run.	• Prefer large teams. • Like well-defined rules and roles. • Need a strong leader who consistently enforces rules and agreements.

The Boomers 1943-1960

"I also do find myself thinking that younger generations ought to "put in their time" as I have. However, as I learn more about the values of the younger generations and the perspective they've gained by watching the "mistakes" that generations before them have made, I look forward to observing their experiment in finding more balance, and perhaps I, too, can learn something from that."—A Baby Boomer posting on www.generationworkplace.com

Values	Assets	Liabilities
• Optimism. • Team orientation. • Personal gratification. • Health and wellness. • Personal growth. • Youth. • Work. • Involvement.	• Service oriented. • Driven. • Willing to "go the extra mile". • Want to please. • Good team players.	• Not naturally "budget minded". • Uncomfortable with conflict. • Overly sensitive to feedback. • Judgmental of those who see things differently. • Self-centered. • Materialistic.

Business Traits	View of Work	Working on Teams
• Need to prove themselves. • Engrossed in their occupations. • Committed to lifelong learning and self-improvement. • People can view them as overly political, self-righteous and self-absorbed.	• Invented the 60-hour work week. • View work as self-fulfillment; a means to prove themselves. • Define selves through career; achieve identity through the work they perform. • Prefer work environments that are democratic, humane and casual.	• Need a meaningful role on the team. • Their need to prove themselves can override commitment to what is best for the team.

Generation X 1960-1980

"As for offering loyalty to employers, I think our generation has seen so many new careers in the technology industry and so many openings to be 'our own boss' that we rebel against the perceived need to have an employer. I don't think that means that we are disloyal to our employers."—A Gen Xer posting on www.Generationworkplace.com

Values	Assets	Liabilities
• Diversity. • Think globally. • Balance. • Technoliteracy. • Informality. • Self-reliance. • Pragmatism. • Personal growth/challenge.	• Adaptable. • Technoliterate. • Independent. • Not intimidated by authority. • Creative. • Goal oriented.	• Impatient. • Poor people skills. • Inexperienced. • Cynical. • Live beyond their means.

Business Traits	View of Work	Working on Teams
• Adept, clever, resourceful, discouraged and disheartened. • Huge distaste for micromanagement. • Sophisticated consumers with Internet savvy. • Seek instant gratification. • Casual approach to authority. • Need to succeed.	• View work as "just a job". • Work to live vs. live to work. • Strive for balance in life and work. • Place a high value on autonomy and independence. • Need supportive working relationships to balance the isolation.	• Team must have a clear mission with well-defined, coherent goals. • Team should provide an opportunity for Xers to learn and grow while contributing to a valuable end-product. • Like to feel "included" in the team, while working independent of the team.

Generation Y/Millennials 1980-2000

"Generation Y is much less likely to respond to the traditional command-and-control type of management still popular in much of today's workforce," says Jordan Kaplan, an associate managerial science professor at Long Island University-Brooklyn in New York. "They've grown up questioning their parents, and now they're questioning their employers. They don't know how to shut up, which is great, but that's aggravating to the 50-year-old manager who says, 'Do it and do it now.'"[xxi]—From a USA Today article on Generation Y, posted online 11/6/2005.

Values	Assets	Liabilities
• Optimism. • Civic duty. • Confidence. • Achievement. • Sociability. • Morality. • Street smarts. • Diversity.	• Collective action. • Optimism. • Tenacity. • Heroic spirit. • Multitasking capabilities. • Technologically savvy. • Resilient. • Want to grow (now).	• Social skills. • Need for supervision and structure. • Inexperience, particularly with handling difficult people issues.

Business Traits	View of Work	Working on Teams
• Curious, they want to know why. • Always seeking numerous mentors. • Manners are key. • Potentially very demanding as they are accustomed to feeling wanted and needed and getting what they want.	• Learning what works. • Goal focused. • Can-do attitude. • Believe hard work and goal setting are the tickets to achieving their dreams. • Hardworking, dedicated and ready to sacrifice personal pleasure for the collective goal.	• Very effective on teams. • Be sure there are well-defined goals. They want to know they will be producing concrete results that meet immediate needs. • Provide structure and direction.

What is next? 2000–

There are many names floating around for the generation born after the millennium. From Generation Z to Digital Natives, society may identify this generation by the technology that is pervasive in their lives.

Generational Perspectives across Cultures

In China, the after-80 generation refers to those born after 1980 and is also sometimes called China's Generation Y. Although the generational designation is the same as in the United States, the outlook on life is different. These people, also called Little Emperors because of the one-child policy in the People's Republic of China, have a different perspective on their country. Growing up in modern China, optimism for the future, newfound excitement for consumerism and entrepreneurship, and acceptance of its historic role in transforming modern China into an economic superpower characterizes this Gen Y group.

In South Korea, the history of the country's democratization identifies the generations that were part of it. For example, the April 19 Generation struggled against the Syngman Rhee regime in 1960, and the 386 Generation witnessed the June 3 uprising in 1987. For these generations, the unification of South and North Korea is a common thread. However, the new generation, the shinsedae, has a much different outlook. The new South Korea nation shapes this generation. This is the first generation of South Koreans who define themselves in terms of the southern part of the peninsula only. Unlike previous generations, they have the least interest in unification

For the most part, generations in India tend to follow a pattern similar to the broad western model, but there are still major differences, especially in the older generations. Many Indians see India's independence in 1947 as marking a generational shift in the country. People born in the 1930s and 1940s tended to be loyal to the new state and to adhere to "traditional" divisions of society. Indian "boomers," those born after independence and into the early 1960s, tended to link success with leaving India and were more suspicious of traditional societal institutions. Generation X saw an improvement in India's economy, and they are more comfortable with diverse perspectives. Generation Y continues this pattern.

Source: http://en.wikipedia.org/wiki/Generation

No matter which generation you belong to, you will be working with and/ or hiring members of these younger generations from across the world. As a Magnetic Leader, you need to understand what they are looking for in an organization, what they can bring to your business and how to engage, empower and enrich them. Since Xers and Millennials are the growing part of the workforce, let us focus on the key items they are looking for.

What do they want from an organization?

- A vision for the future.

- Vision as it relates to them, broken down into deliverables.

- Understanding how the company's products create a better world.

- Specific milestones.

- Flexible work schedules.

- Competitive salaries.

- Great benefits.

- Access to information.

- A positive work environment that respects balance.

What do they want from managers?

- Leadership they respect and admire.

- Collaborative team environment.

- Opportunities to grow and develop.

- Gaining experience from range of projects.

- Regular constructive feedback and recognition.

- Support and guidance without micromanagement.

What recruitment techniques will work to attract them?

- Candid conversation.

- Casual culture.

- Internship programs.

- Web site.

- Description of growth opportunities.

- Training programs.

- How the company's products create a better world.

A Look at Generation Y and Money

These statistics are from a USA Today article published April 23, 2010. I think what is important to put in context is that this generation's perspective on money will change and evolve as the economy does. So, looking at them as the "debtor generation" could be premature. We still need to see how they will handle the debt that many incur to go to college.

- About 37 percent of 18- to 29-year-olds have been underemployed or out of work during the recession, the highest percentage among that age group in more than three decades, according to a Pew Research Center study released in February 2010.

- This generation is the least likely of any to have health insurance coverage. Just 61 percent say they have a health plan, the Pew study said.

- Only 58 percent pay monthly bills on time, according to a National Foundation for Credit Counseling (NFCC) 2010 survey.

- Sixty percent of workers 20- to 29-years-old cashed out their 401k retirement plans—typically a big financial no-no because such a move squanders retirement assets and forces the recipient to pay a tax penalty—when they changed or lost jobs, an October study by Hewitt Associates said.

- Nearly 70 percent of Gen Y members are not building up a cash cushion, and 43 percent are amassing too much credit-card debt, according to a November MetLife poll.

- On average, Gen Yers each have more than three credit cards, and 20 percent carry a balance of more than $10,000, according to Fidelity Investments.

- Millennials are graduating from college with an average of $23,200 in student debt, according to the most recent data from the Project on Student Debt. That is a 24-percent increase from 2004.

Source: 4/23/10 Usatoday.com
http://www.usatoday.com/money/economy/2010-04-23-1Ageny23_CV_N.htm

Test your Team's Generation IQ

After you have reviewed the generational information with your team, divide people into groups where there is as much age diversity as possible. Then ask the groups questions about each generation and keep score as to which group answers the most questions right.

Here are 10 questions to get you started:

1. **Which two generations value civic pride?**
2. **Which generation invented the 60-hour work week?**
3. **Which generation has the greatest multi-tasking ability?**
4. **Which generation is adaptable?**
5. **Which generation believes in duty before pleasure?**
6. **Which generation is very effective on teams?**
7. **Which generation cannot tolerate micro-management?**
8. **Which generation defines itself by career?**
9. **Which generation is seeking numerous mentors?**
10. **Which generation needs a strong leader that consistently enforces rules and agreements?**

Answers:

1. Veterans and Generation Y.
2. Baby Boomers.
3. Generation Y.
4. Generation X.
5. Veterans.
6. Generation Y.
7. Generation X and Generation Y.
8. Baby Boomers.
9. Generation Y.
10. Veterans.

A R.E.A.L. Tip

No generation is superior to another. Each generation can learn and benefit from the strengths of another. Coupling the generations in the workplace transfers the expertise and knowledge.

The Triple Bottom-Line in Generational Context

People. Planet. Profit. The three pillars of sustainability. While this might sound Utopian to someone from the Veteran generation, think of Generation X and Y who have pushed the conversation about environmental responsibility forward and who also have more at stake for the future health of the planet.

With access to the Internet, Gen X and Y are the ones who look closely at corporate responsibility and want to know what is behind the large check the community receives. They question corporate responsibility more than the generations before them. While their grandparents thought of corporate responsibility as a pension, these generations are thinking about it in the context of the environment and making the world a better place.

When you develop your corporate responsibility programs and policies, think from the perspective of your engaged employees as well as your customers. How would a Generation Y candidate judge you? What is your track record for giving back and impacting the triple bottom line? What is your reputation when it comes to how you treat your employees?

In this chapter, we looked at the importance of appreciation, rewards and recognition and gave examples of how you can make appreciation a part of your Magnetic Leadership strategy. Now let us look at how the whole picture comes together to create leadership that leads to loyalty.

Chapter Six
Creating Value and Loyalty through Leadership

"I'll take fifty percent efficiency to get one hundred percent loyalty."

—Samuel Goldwyn

By now, I hope you can clearly see the picture of Magnetic Leadership that I have been painting. You see it is not a purely solo endeavor. You see that leadership requires compassion, understanding and conviction. You see how important trust, participation, mentorship and coaching are in the process. You see the power of the Es (engagement, empowerment, enrichment and environment).

And you see how without appreciation, rewards and recognition, the painting is flat. It is unfinished.

Without Magnetic Leadership, loyalty of customers and employees is simply not possible.

There is a lot of focus today on leadership style. And what I have seen as I work with successful CEOs over the years is that they all have one thing in common: they are willing to make tough decisions to benefit the organization and move it forward. No matter what their leadership style is, they focus on doing whatever it takes to make their organizations better. They put their personal issues and egos aside for the benefit of the organization. Magnetic Leadership focuses more on leadership traits and less on style.

First, we need to reexamine the traits of outstanding leaders. Then we can look at leadership in action before exploring the role that personal energy has to play. Finally, I will look at how being a healthy leader plays an important role in Magnetic Leadership.

Traits of Magnetic Leaders

Sets the challenge

- Creates and communicates a vision or goal that compels others.
- Sets a positive tone through energy and optimism.

Engages people in the possibilities

- Speaks to the possibilities in a clear and concise fashion.
- Articulates the vision or goal with clarity and understanding.
- Leads by example.

Creates trust

- Encourages others to take risks through honesty, integrity, openness and reliability.
- Sets a positive tone by never doubting people.
- Gets others to want to do things instead of having to ask them.

Distributes power

- Shares decision making.
- Gives credit where credit is due.
- Values innovation.

Knows self and others

- Understands their own and others' strengths and weaknesses.
- Believes anyone can achieve what they set their mind to.
- Looks for the people of promise and passion in their organizations.

Dianne M. Durkin with Carey Earle

Celebrates successes

- Recognizes performance, rewards results.

- Celebrates the small achievements on the road to the larger goal.

- Celebrates what people learn from failures or failed attempts.

The Role of Communication in Leadership

Communication is at the heart of leadership. Think of communication as the connective tissue that makes Magnetic Leadership possible. Everything from purpose and vision to accountability cannot work without communication. The engagement and empowerment I spoke of in chapter four cannot happen without it. People need to know you value their input and want their creativity and innovative ideas to solve business problems. The message is, "you have brains, and we want you to use them."

Look at what a Magnetic Leadership environment communicates:

- Clarity of purpose, vision and values.

- Direct, honest and developmental feedback.

- Accountability and responsibility.

- Customized recognition and rewards.

- Ongoing acts of appreciation.

- Goal setting at both individual and organizational levels.

In order for communication to be authentic, what you are communicating has to be alive and well. In a Magnetic Leadership environment, you and your team are modeling:

- Trust.

- Flexibility.

- Openness to creativity and innovation.

- Fairness.

- Whatever values you identified as core to your organization.

Let us look at Magnetic Leadership in action. First, I want to start with an organization where I have personally experienced Magnetic Leadership.

Spotlight on The Edgewood Centre, Portsmouth, N.H.

My father lived at this family-owned, long-term care facility, so I have seen firsthand the level of care and compassion at play on every level of this organization. The Edgewood Centre employs over 200 people and is a 156-bed facility that offers both long-term care and rehabilitation services.

Patricia Ramsey became its sole owner in 2003 after taking the business over in the mid-80s with her brother. At the time she and her brother took the reins, the organization's reputation was "not the best," and Patricia knew she had a lot of work ahead of her.

Her goal? Creating an environment where families want to place their relatives and where people living in the area want to work.

A focus on the work environment

Over the years, Ramsey and her team developed numerous programs to create a supportive environment for both employees and residents. All of these programs bring the centre's values to life.

> ### Edgewood Centre Values
>
> The staff and residents of the Edgewood Centre have joined together to establish a set of values that describes the heart of how they want to live and work together. These values are intended as guiding principles which serve to build a foundation of caring. They ask all who live and work at the facility to strive to uphold these values.
>
> #### Home
>
> We believe in creating an environment that we, ourselves would want to call home – a home filled with family, friends, spontaneity, normalcy and joy.
>
> #### Empowerment
>
> For the residents, we believe in honoring individual choices and in the right to exercise control over decisions and daily routines. For the

staff, we seek a working environment that places decision making closest to the resident and values suggestion and individual initiative.

Appreciation

We believe in the importance of acknowledging each person's accomplishments with personal expressions of congratulations and gratitude.

Relationship

We believe that Relationship is the heart of long-term care. What makes Edgewood a special place to live and work is the quality of the relationships that we form between the staff, residents, children and visitors. These relationships are based upon the simple power of kindness, respect, forgiveness and honesty.

Teamwork

We believe that by working as a team we will achieve a consistently high standard of quality of care and quality of life. We will support each other's efforts and hold each other accountable to uphold these guiding principles.

The above material is excerpted with permission from "The Edgewood Centre: Aligning Values and Business Strategy," The Business of Caregiving, a series of case studies published by the Paraprofessional Healthcare Institute, 2010 (www.PHInational.org) with funding from the Hitachi Foundation. PHI has worked with the Edgewood leadership, managers, and direct-care staff to create a culture that delivers quality relationships centered care, and respecting and empowering staff and residents.

"It's about doing the right thing," says Ramsey. "I've got to feel good when I come to work every day, and I want the people that I work with to feel the same. Because in the end, if they're not happy, our residents are not going to be happy."

Caring for families

One of the first programs Ramsey developed specifically to address worker retention was an on-site, day-care center. Edgewood's day-care center, now called the Learning Center, opened in 1985. A survey of staff, which included many single mothers, brought childcare to the top of their list of desired support, and Edgewood leadership moved quickly to convert two teaching rooms into childcare classrooms. A very successful recruitment tool, The Learning Center is now open to other families in the region.

The Edgewood Centre fosters a family environment and promotes inter-generational activities that encourage interaction between the children and the elders: Children visit with residents throughout the week and join them for exercise groups, craft activities and parties, including a recent pre-school graduation party.

Providing opportunities for growth

To cultivate a positive Edgewood culture, Edgewood leadership deliberately looks for opportunities to promote from within. "If a person demonstrates competence, and they are truly a person who has bought into the Edgewood way of life in terms of our culture, our philosophy, our way of doing things, and there is an opportunity for growth, we feel they deserve that opportunity," states Ramsey. In fact, three current department heads began their careers at Edgewood as licensed nursing assistants (LNAs).

Edgewood supports many of its LNAs to participate in the State of New Hampshire's MedTech licensing program, a career ladder the state created for direct-care staff. MedTechs administer oral, non-controlled medications under the supervision of a licensed nurse. MedTechs also receive an hourly wage increase upon completion of a three-week intensive training course. Aside from MedTechs, Edgewood offers several career-ladder opportunities, including peer mentor, specialty-aide positions and LNA team leader.

Building and empowering communities of staff and residents

Edgewood, like other organizations on the path of culture change, restructured itself into communities in 2007 in the interest of creating a more home-like, resident-centered environment where residents and those working closest with them are involved in decision making. Edgewood defines a community as an area with a country kitchen and approximately 30 bedrooms. Each community has a consistent group of staff working with and for the same group of residents.

Shifting decision making to the community level required good communication skills and a certain amount of "letting go" on the part of senior leadership – they have to trust that community leaders and team members can work through problems. And the effort has paid off.

"It's amazing the level of decision making that's going on at the community level and at the resident level," notes Ramsey. "It's because all the caregivers – the LNAs, the nurses, the social worker, the recreation staff and the dietary aide who is now called a life enhancer – are a whole team of people supporting decision making with the residents. It has enabled the management staff to be doing more things that we all need to be doing such as looking at the macro-level, and how we're going to stay competitive and be more proactive than reactive."

Following the shift to a community structure, Edgewood took on the challenge of consistent assignments. In this model, residents receive care from the same caregivers from day to day. Consistent assignments benefit the caregiver, the residents and their families. It provides the opportunity to establish routines, to nurture relationships, to notice changes and to provide consistent information. Edgewood asked residents and workers with whom they would like to work and paired accordingly.

Consistent assignment also has meant greater family satisfaction. Ramsey reports that family members repeatedly express appreciation knowing they can communicate with the LNA who works directly with their relative and also having the assurance that the LNA knows their relative well.

Establishing systems for good communication and supervisory support

Ramsey saw a need for greater sustainability of the programs they created. As previously discussed, if there is not consistency, you cannot have lasting results. So, Ramsey saw coaching as part of the solution.

Pat Cummings, admissions director, explains, "Our philosophy is that when supervisors can develop a deeper relationship with an employee and empower employees to solve their own problems – that employee actually has a better answer nine times out of 10 than the supervisor. Then there's more ownership around the issue, and ultimately, that ownership translates into commitment and loyalty."

And what has the pay off been for their Magnetic Leadership? Increased satisfaction of both employees and residents, the creation of a family environment that truly delivers the best care at every level and higher levels of employee retention.

The state of New Hampshire also has recognized their work. For three years in a row, Edgewood has won the New Hampshire Department of Health and Human Services' "Quality of Life" award, which recognizes quality-of-life initiatives and improvements at nursing homes across the state, including resident empowerment, resident care and choice, home environment and community involvement.

Now let us travel across the country and change the leadership lens from a small business in New England to a global corporation in California.

Sony Pictures, Culver City, CA[xxii]

With 6,300 employees worldwide, Sony Pictures produces, markets and distributes movies and TV shows. The co-chairs of Sony Pictures, Michael Lynton and Amy Pascal wanted to create a highly engaged, employee-friendly and high-performance culture. They engaged Tony Schwartz of The Energy Project.[xxiii]

The first place they focused was on making two fundamental shifts in the way Sony managed its employees.

1. **Employees are not computers. Though we live in a culture where technology is pervasive, human beings still do not work like computers. We cannot operate at high speeds continuously, running multiple programs at once.**

2. **Get more by demanding less. Instead of trying to get more out of employees, focus on meeting their four core needs.**

   - Physical health (nutrition, sleep, daytime renewal and exercise).

   - Emotional well-being (appreciated and rewarded).

   - Mental clarity (the ability to focus intensely, prioritize and think creatively).

   - Spiritual significance (the feeling of serving a mission beyond generating a profit).

After getting buy-in at senior levels, Tony Schwartz' team then developed specific energy-management practices to improve both personal effectiveness and leadership. These are rituals that refuel energy and ultimately allow for intense focus for specific periods of time. This is because of the premise that people perform at their peak when they alternate between periods of intense focus and renewal.

Examples of intermittent renewal to replenish energy

- Take a brisk walk in the afternoon to get a breather from the office.

- Turn off e-mail for a period of time each day so you can focus and tackle high priorities.

- Get away from your desk for lunch, and encourage your employees to do the same.

- Create an informal, relaxing space that is for creative thinking and brainstorming.

- Show appreciation to those around you, and let them know they are valued.

It is important to take the time to identify anything in your organization that may be draining energy. For example, are you avoiding conflict and creating tension? Do people feel like they are always on and never have down time?

Sony discovered that e-mail was an issue of stress and tension. People felt they had to reply to e-mails in the evenings and on weekends. They felt they were always on call, and they could not let go of work. This created resentment and was clearly an energy drain. The team agreed on an 8 a.m. to 8 p.m. weekday limit – outside of those hours, they were free not to respond to e-mail with the understanding that anything urgent would warrant a phone call.

As part of this energy-renewal program, Sony converted a sound stage where staff can take yoga classes, have a fitness or nutrition consultation or a massage. Sony Pictures also started subsidizing healthy meals and a salad bar at an on-site restaurant for employees. They also built a new gym and created a grassy commons area where people can relax. To recharge on the spiritual level, Sony also offers its employees paid time off each month to volunteer and organizes volunteer opportunities that teams can do.

While the team at Sony Pictures sees these changes as a beginning, they recognize they developed a common language around energy and people's core needs.

"This has been about believing that the culture of the company is as important as the product," said Amy Pascal, co-chair of Sony Pictures.

To date, 3,000 of Sony Picture's employees have gone through this energy-management program. Eighty-eight percent of participants say it made them more focused and productive. Ninety percent say it helped them bring more energy to work. Eighty-four percent say they feel better able to manage their jobs' demands and their work engages them.

What has been the impact to the bottom-line? Despite the recession, Sony had its most profitable year in 2008 and one of its highest-revenue years in 2009.

"…There's no question that this investment we've made in our employees has energized and motivated them and helped us stay strong in the midst of very tough times," said Pascal.

Source: The Productivity Paradox. How Sony Pictures Gets More Out of People by Demanding Less. By Tony Schwartz. Harvard Business Review. June 2010.

This inspirational copy is on Sony's corporate web site, and I could not help but think how achievable this purpose statement is with the work Sony Pictures is doing with The Energy Project.

We Help Dreamers Dream

Sony is a company devoted to the CELEBRATION of life. We create things for every kind of IMAGINATION. Products that stimulate the SENSES and refresh the spirit. Ideas that always surprise and never disappoint. INNOVATIONS that are easy to love, and EFFORTLESS to use, things that are not essential, yet hard to live without.

We are not here to be logical. Or predictable. We're here to pursue INFINITE possibilities. We allow the BRIGHTEST minds to interact freely, so the UNEXPECTED can emerge. We invite new THINKING so even more fantastic ideas can evolve. CREATIVITY is our essence. We take chances. We EXCEED expectations. We help dreamers DREAM.

Source: http://news.sel.sony.com/en/corporate_information/sony_brand

---

The Chief Energy Officer

You can see how energy is a powerful catalyst for change and can be one of a leader's greatest tools to connect leadership to loyalty. In Jon Gordon's international bestseller, "The Energy Bus," he says that CEO stands for Chief Energy Officer.

"Why energy? Because energy is the currency of personal and professional success today. If you don't have it, you can't lead, inspire or make a difference. And the great thing about being a Chief Energy Officer is that anyone in your company, including you, can become one. Deciding to become a Chief Energy Officer means that you share positive, powerful and contagious energy with your co-workers, employees and customers! It means that you communicate from the heart."

Here are the 10 Rules that Gordon offers in "The Energy Bus":

1. **You are the driver of your bus.** Take responsibility for your life and control your bus, so you can get where you want to go.

2. **Desire, vision and focus move your bus in the right direction.** The more we think about something, focus on something, the more it shows up in our lives. The good old law of attraction.

3. **Fuel your ride with positive energy.** Every day when we look at the gas pump of life, we have a choice between positive energy and negative energy.

4. **Invite people on your bus and share your vision for the road ahead.** You cannot accomplish your goals if you are the only person on the bus. You need the support of your team.

5. **Do not waste your energy on those who do not get on your bus.** Give your energy to the people who are already on your bus.

6. **Post a sign on your bus that says NO ENERGY VAMPIRES ALLOWED.** Kick those with toxic attitudes off the bus.

7. **Enthusiasm attracts more passengers and energizes them during the ride.** Remember when your grandma or grandpa said you can attract more bees with honey than vinegar?

8. **Love your passengers.** Being recognized and feeling that someone cares is a basic human need. Group hug, anybody?

9. **Drive with purpose.** Here is the P word again! Without purpose, no one gets anything done. The bus stalls.

10. **Have fun and enjoy the ride.** This is what I call "putting the top down." If you are not having fun, what is the point?

We have all heard the bus analogy before. Jim Collins used it in "From Good to Great" when he reminded us to "Get the right people on the bus." We have all sung a rousing chorus of "The Wheels on the Bus Go 'Round and 'Round" at some point in our lives. The reason people often repeat this analogy is because it makes sense. Everyone can relate to a bus. It is a simple concept without corporate jargon, and using the bus as a metaphor makes business ideas and concepts accessible to everyone.

Also, getting a sense of the energy in your company is not difficult. It is palpable. What does it feel like when you walk into your offices, factory floors, retail stores? What is the vibe? Do you feel better having been there? If the answer is no, then you need to look at each letter in the R.E.A.L. approach, and see where your Magnetic Leadership force fields are weak.

Is It in the **R** – Recruiting and retention efforts?

Is it in the **E** – Employee engagement, empowerment, enrichment and environment?

Is it in the **A** – Appreciating, rewarding or recognizing your employees?

Is it in the **L** – Cultivating a culture of leadership with energy that is contagious?

At different times in your organization, you may find you are focusing more attention on one area than another, and this is normal. The key is to watch each area and watch the indicators in your business – both the financial numbers as well as your employee and customer-satisfaction metrics. Think about the people behind the profit. They are always the key to turning things around.

A R.E.A.L. Tip

There is profit and there is people, and you cannot have one without the other.

Do Healthy Leaders Run Healthier Companies?

Mike Goldsby, a management professor at Ball State University's Miller College of Business, teamed up with Dr. Donald Karatko, founding director of the business school's entrepreneurship program at Ball State, and James Bishop from New Mexico State University looked at how many of the CEOs in their study were fanatical runners or weightlifters. They also asked how satisfied the CEOs were with their jobs and how their companies were doing financially. The study included more than 360 small-business executives from Indiana and neighboring states.

They were researching correlations between fitness practices and business and personal success. The answer was a resounding **YES** to there being a relationship. They found the runners and weightlifters had both higher personal job satisfaction and greater financial gains. They also found the CEOs who were runners were more successful in terms of sales than the non-running CEOs.

Respondents also reported their success levels increased once they began running or weightlifting. Goldsby has some theories about the link between fitness and success. One is that the work ethic spills over from the gym to the workplace. The person who can get up and work out when she does not feel like it is the same kind of person who will not give up on a problem and will keep working on it. Another possibility is that fitness enthusiasts tend to look better, and we humans tend to factor looks into all of our decisions, including business decisions.

Source: Indiana Business Magazine, August 1, 2004. Fiscal Fitness? Can CEO's exercise habits improve company sales? By Steve Kaelble.

An important thing to remember as a leader is if your team sees you take the time to exercise, it also gives them permission to step away from the computer and go workout. Let us look at some CEOs and their exercise routines.

A R.E.A.L. Tip

Think about what your exercise and health behavior communicates or models to your team.

Snapshots of CEO exercise routines

Pat O'Donnell, CEO of Aspen Skiing Company

He starts every day with an early morning workout at the Snowmass Club. He says, "That's when I do a lot of my thinking. As a matter of fact, it's almost ridiculous now because I take a little notepad from station to station, and I usually walk out with six or seven new ideas every morning."

Elizabeth Curtis, CEO of Sharp Community Medical Group, the second-largest employer in San Diego

She works out at the gym every morning during the week, timed to miss the traffic. On the weekends, she rides horses, bikes, water skis, chops wood and works in her garden.

Source: Fit to be CEO: how some CEOs link fitness and performance. Chief Executive magazine. September 1, 2006. By Peter McLaughlin (www.petermclaughlin.com).

Larry Ellison, CEO Oracle Corp

Ellison is an experienced yachtsman. He won the Maxi-World Championships five times on his boat Sayonara and earned the number-two slot skippering the BMW-Oracle team in the 2009 American's Cup. He sails on his 452-foot yacht, Rising Sun, which is said to be the world's largest personal yacht.

Julie Smolyansky, CEO Lifeway Foods, Morton Grove, Ill.

She starts the day with a glass of kefir, the probiotic dairy drink that Lifeway is famous for. She rides her bicycle between 40 and 60 miles a week. She also runs six miles, three days a week, lifts weights and kick boxes

Sir Richard Branson, CEO Virgin Group, Britain

Branson water skis, windsurfs and kite-surfs, which is a hybrid of paragliding and windsurfing. In 1987, he crossed the Atlantic in the world's largest hot-air balloon, the Virgin Atlantic Flyer, and broke the balloon speed record crossing the Pacific Ocean from Japan to Arctic Canada.

Sky Dayton, CEO SK-Earthlink and founder of ISP Earthlink and Boingo Wireless, Santa Monica, California.

An avid snowboarder and self-described surfaholic, Dayton rides the waves off the California coast, Fiji, Indonesia and Hawaii. He surfs for an hour and half every morning before he goes to his San Diego office.

Source: Business Week: Fittest CEO's
http://images.businessweek.com/ss/05/08/fittestceos/source/2.htm

Think about what is at stake when a workplace is not healthy and does not encourage healthy lifestyles. According to a study conducted by Mercer,[xxiv] during an average workday of 11.9 hours, 73 percent of the senior executives surveyed were physically inactive, 40 percent were obese and 75 percent had two or more risk factors for cardiovascular disease. What is the cost of that to an organization? And by cost, I am talking about more than health care—the loss of the expertise and the thinking.

Part of your Magnetic Leadership strategy is to lower stress for yourself and everyone in your organization. Research conducted in Sweden from 1992–2003,[xxv] clearly showed those participants who were suppressing anger or "gulping down" emotions were more likely to have a heart attack. The researchers found those who handled conflict by suppressing their anger and not saying anything had double the risk for heart attack or cardiac death, and for those that held their anger inside and suffered physical distress later, the risk was triple.

You now can see that so many aspects of our R.E.A.L. strategy are not just good business, they are also part of good health.

R When you recruit and retain the right people, you are not creating a stressful environment by trying to fit square pegs in round holes.

E When you engage, empower and enrich employees, you give them the tools to be happier people who perform at their best and live whole lives.

A When people feel appreciated, they are not angry, divisive or dismissive to others.

L When you model Magnetic Leadership, you create a communicative and collaborative environment where people can be happy and healthy.

In this chapter, I talked about the Power of Magnetic Leadership in every level of your organization; what it did for a long-term care company in New Hampshire and how it is shifting the energy in Sony Pictures. We looked at the connection between the health of an organization and the health of CEOs. Now let us look ahead and think about what the future of leadership might hold.

Chapter Seven
Leadership in a Complex Changing World

> *"It's not fair to ask of others what you*
> *are not willing to do yourself."*
>
> —*Eleanor Roosevelt*

What does Magnetic Leadership look like in a workforce that becomes even more virtual? We saw how important communication is in the R.E.A.L. approach. Let us think about how the importance of communication increases as teams are more cross-cultural, cross time-zone and working in "pods" around the world. In a virtual work place, consistent and authentic communication is the lifeblood of the organization. The leader who does not communicate well, does not engage people. Period.

When to Skype or not to Skype

With the pervasiveness of technology, tomorrow's leaders definitely need to be much more tech savvy than the leaders of today. They also need to make decisions about when to be hi-tech or hi-touch.

- When do they need to bring people together in person? When will Skype or Gotomeeting just not cut it?

- How will they communicate even better with all the technology at their command?

- How will they gain trust in an organization where many employees may never or rarely see them?

When Whirlpool CEO Jeff M. Fettig looks at the future and how leaders will need to lead, here is what he has to say:

"Our business is not just driven by the United States anymore. We are operating in a truly global economy in which volatility and the speed of change have radically increased. We are moving from a plan-forecast-and-deploy model to a read-and-react model. You cannot predict a lot of this stuff. At the same time, you need to be good at reading market signals and reacting really fast."

Jurgen Hambrecht, Chairman of the Board of Executive Directors, sees social responsibility as key in the future.

"I think industry needs to raise its voice more. There is the temptation to lean toward protectionism and bureaucracy, especially in Europe. We need to have the freedom to operate, and we need to explain why this is important to the public. Industry leaders have to be more outspoken. We need to jointly speak out and recognize that we have a responsibility beyond the company—a social responsibility. I think we need to improve in this area."

Indra K. Nooyi, Chairman and Chief Executive Officer, PepsiCo, sees the importance of watching for growth patterns to shift globally.

"If you look around the world, there's still growth, but we have to view our portfolio differently. Although developed markets may not grow as fast as they have in the past, developing and emerging markets will grow faster. We have to make sure people understand that growth patterns will shift. We also must give people the opportunity to work in international markets if they're so inclined and have the capability."

Source: The Future of Leadership. Conversations with Leaders about their Challenges. Boston Consulting Group. April 2010. http://leadership.bcg.com/images/file42391.pdf

In all the comments above, the leaders reference change and adaptability. When I think about Magnetic Leadership, part of the power it has is the ability to change and adapt by connecting with engaged employees. By understanding the generational differences in the changing workforce and getting the right people in the right place at the right time, you are creating a team with the energy to address change. Change is only possible with engaged employees. That makes Magnetic Leadership necessary now and in the future.

When I think about a leader of the future, I see someone who:

- Is a strong communicator both in person and electronically.
- Embraces adaptation and change.
- Has respect for all people from all cultures.
- Values ideas from throughout the organization.

- Values cultural and generational differences.

- Sees the world as a global citizen.

- Embraces social responsibility and philanthropy.

- Cultivates a healthy work environment.

- Looks at the whole person (like the Balanced Wheel of Success).

- Is probably not wearing a suit.

- Speaks more than one language or has an application for that.

Tomorrow's leaders will experience life in a time where change continues to accelerate. Scenario planning like Peter Schwartz discusses in his book "The Art of the Long View" will become more important. Schwartz sees "rehearsing for the future" as a key part of leadership in a changing world. He outlines eight steps to guide leaders to always proactively plan and think ahead.

Step 1: Identify the focal issue or decision.
What is keeping you up at night?
What are the key issues in your industry and in your organization?

Step 2: Identify the key forces in the local environment.
What will decision makers want to know when making key choices?
What will success or failure be?
What are the considerations that will shape these outcomes?

Step 3: Identify driving forces.
What are the macro forces behind the forces listed in step two?

Step 4: Rank by importance and uncertainty.
To what degree is the success of the focal issue or decision identified in step one important?
What is the degree of uncertainty surrounding factors and trends?
The point is to identify the two or three factors or trends that are most important and most uncertain.

Step 5: Create scenario logic.
Map out plausible scenarios.

Step 6: Flesh out the scenarios.
What are the five Ws (Who, What, Where, When, Why,) and How?

Dianne M. Durkin with Carey Earle

Step 7: What are the implications?

How does the decision look in each scenario?

What vulnerabilities do you see?

Is the decision or strategy good in all scenarios, just one scenario, a few? If it is good in only one or two of several scenarios, consider it high risk.

Step 8: Decide, select leading indicators, signposts and adjustment plans.

A R.E.A.L. Tip

Think about how you can rehearse for your organization's future.

When you look at Schwartz's eight steps, you can see how important Magnetic Leadership is. No one individual can create a powerful future scenario alone. It takes expertise from throughout the organization. It can only happen in an organization where there is trust and where leadership has spread throughout the ranks.

A solo leader cannot predict or envision the future sitting alone in a room. The future leader needs a powerful network of leaders all over the world. She will know how to effectively tap those leaders and gather expertise quickly to solve problems.

Trina Soske and Jay A. Conger captured the importance of the team versus the individual leader in a Harvard Business Review blog called Imagining the Future of Leadership.[xxvi]

"The complexity, interconnectedness and transparency of today's organizations mean that no one individual can get much accomplished by themselves. Most challenges and opportunities are systemic. Leadership is distributed and change now requires a collective sense and a coordinated set of actions."

Soske and Conger also cite the danger of "the great man theory" is that it focuses leadership on attributes alone versus issues. Left over from the industrial economy and nostalgic imagery of John Wayne-style saviors, many organizations still want to believe in the one hero who rides in and saves the day. However, in a complex global economy, one horse and one man no longer makes sense. To solve complex issues, you need the best brains at the table. You want a lot of horses with riders from different backgrounds and perspectives.

Charles J. Palus discusses the shift from leader to leadership in his post on the Harvard Business Review blog entitled, A Declaration of Interdependence.

"The interdependent companies we've studied have expanded from an exclusive focus on leader development, which is about character, competence, quantity of individuals in defined roles, to leadership development, which is the expansion of a collective's shared beliefs and practices for creating direction, alignment and commitment (DAC). Leadership development, in other words, targets the leadership culture of the organization. DAC, we have found, is produced by dependent, independent, or interdependent leadership cultures."

He sees DAC as core to the future health of leadership.

- **Direction:** how will we decide where to go?

- **Alignment:** how will we coordinate our work?

- **Commitment:** how will we stay engaged and accountable?

Source: http://blogs.hbr.org/imagining-the-future-of-leadership/2010/06/a-declaration-of-interdependen.html#comments

Beyond Business Experience

PepsiCo CEO Indra Nooyi thinks that for CEOs of the future, pure business experience will not be enough. She sees time spent working in government or non-governmental organizations (NGO)[xxvii] as critical—since government and governmental regulation is a key issue for any leader. This supports what IBM is doing with its Corporate Service Corps.

Here is how IBM describes The Corporate Service Corps (CSC) on its web site: "CSC exposes high-performance IBM employees to the 21st century context for doing business -- emerging markets, global teaming, diverse cultures, working outside the traditional office and increased societal expectations for more responsible and sustainable business practices. CSC participants perform community-driven economic development projects in Africa, Asia, Eastern Europe and Latin America, working at the intersection of business, technology and society."

Source: https://www-146.ibm.com/corporateservicecorps/

Since IBM launched this program in July 2008, the CSC has deployed 500 IBM employees from 44 countries on 29 teams to nine countries. Their projects range from assisting networks of entrepreneurs and small businesses trying to grow using information technology to communities left behind by "the digital divide."

IBM has taken the John F. Kennedy dream of the Peace Corps and applied it to business. Sounds like IBM embraces the Balanced Wheel of Success. They see leadership as developing the whole person.

Look at benefits of IBM's Corporate Service Corps:

- They develop talent in a better, faster and cheaper way.

- Employees experience working across cultures in radically different business contexts and in a hands-on way.

- Society benefits as local non-profits get the expertise of highly skilled workers they could never afford to hire.

- Corporate reputation increases locally; IBM is seen as a company that "gets" the local culture, cares about that community's businesses, infrastructure and people, and builds its credibility for future business opportunities.

- Employee retention and engagement increases as IBM workers take pride in their company's investment in themselves and in society at large.

Here are a few examples of other corporations using similar models.

- Cisco has a Leadership Fellows Program that places senior managers in NGOs around the world.

- Pfizer's Global Health Fellows Program provides assistance to local anti-HIV organizations.

- Accenture has a cross-volunteering program that is part of its management consulting practice. They describe it as a market-based approach to help NGO clients access Accenture's talent.

Source: From Corporate University to Corps by Daisy Wademan Dowling and Matthew Breifelder. http://blogs.hbr.org/imagining-the-future-of-leadership/2010/06/from-corporate-university-to-c-1. html

If we think back to Generation Y's more global perspective on life and culture, these kinds of programs fit nicely with how the upcoming generations may view their role as global citizens who should give back. This is a strength of Generation Y since having a "global mindset" is important to them. Of course, "global mindset" means different things to different people. Here is how one professor defines it.

Mansour Javidan, the Dean of Research, Garvin Distinguished Professor, and Director of the Global Mindset Leadership at Thunderbird School of Global Management, sees three keys to having a global mindset[xxviii]:"

1. **Intellectual capital:** global business savvy, cognitive complexity, cosmopolitan outlook.

2. **Psychological capital:** passion for diversity, quest for adventure, self-assurance.

3. **Social capital:** intercultural empathy, interpersonal impact, diplomacy.

Views on Leadership May Change from Country to Country

As an educator, Javidan sees the role of universities as critical in helping their students develop global mindsets. However, he cautions, we must remember that from country to country, the view of leadership changes. For example, he shares this perspective on the best leaders from a survey of Chinese managers[xxix]:

The best leaders:

- Are friends with their subordinates.

- Make decisions on their own.

- Compete with their own direct reports and make sure they are better than others.

- Speak honestly, while taking into account others' status.

- Use indirect language and metaphors rather than get straight to the point.

- Avoid taking risks.

American or European leaders would see this definition as odd or out of sync with their own experiences. The point is that we throw the word "global" around, and we need to make sure we think of the implications when we are leading. Magnetic Leadership is about understanding differences and recognizing that in today's workforce there is no such thing as one size fits all.

With all of our differences though, there are still universal themes that cross cultures. And in its simplest form, that universality is around "doing well" or "doing what is right." If you think of iconic figures like Gandhi or Martin Luther King, they moved people because they stood for what they believed was right. As a Magnetic Leader, you also need to be ready to do what is right by all of your stakeholders—not only your shareholders.

Today, people can praise or parody leaders to millions in a few minutes on YouTube or in the Blogosphere. Social media allows people to immediately decide whether to critique or congratulate you on your good deeds and bad. It will be "old hat" to tomorrow's leaders that the next star in their organization may be the "under the radar" employee with a Twitter following of 500,000 or the community activist who has engaged a million people on Facebook. That is why as a Magnetic Leader you want to be proud of every action you and your team take.

Tomorrow's leader will accept the transparency of social media and also see the value of its authenticity and democracy. Like the Internet, the social networks will reflect the best and worst of our culture. Tomorrow's leader also will ultimately face the same choice as you do today: what kind of leader are you going to be?

As you think about the future of leadership for yourself, zoom in on today. In our final chapter, we look at the action steps you can take now to become a R.E.A.L. leader.

Chapter Eight
Top-10 Checklist for Magnetic Leadership

You made it to last chapter, or maybe you are reading the ending first. Either way, we know we all live in a sound-bite world, and we have the desire to read the cliff notes or at the very least to be able to digest the key points quickly. So let us look at the **Top Ten Checklist for Magnetic Leadership.**

1. **Got vision?** Make sure you have a vision with the purpose and values to make it real. Without a clear vision, you cannot pass go and grow your revenue. Go back to chapter one if you have the vision blues.

2. **What kind of leader are you?** Authentic leadership is about trust and knowing who you are as a leader. Take the assessments in chapter two to figure out where to focus your efforts.

3. **How to keep yourself on track?** Keep a leadership log, as discussed in chapter two, and regularly reflect on what you are learning and how you are changing. Think of it as your sixth-grade journal without the Scooby Doo stickers.

4. **Are you recruiting the right people and retaining tomorrow's rock stars?** Make sure you have identified the people you need to make your vision a reality. You cannot always meet tomorrow's goals with yesterday's team. Retaining people is about knowing what they want and building a culture that keeps them happy. Cruise back to chapter three if you need to improve your interview process or fine tune your listening skills so you can hear what your employees are saying.

5. **Are your employees engaged in your company's vision, empowered to be part of the change and enriched by your culture?** It is not a tall order when you break it down. The most important rule to remember is to make your employees part of building solutions and implementing them. Ownership comes from participation and understanding where you are going. Chapter four is the Big E for a reason -- without engagement, empowerment and enrichment, your company is losing the best employees and possibly the next big idea.

6. **Do you have a work environment that fosters creativity and innovation?** I am not saying you have to have bean-bag chairs and lava lamps – the physical environment is just one element. Think about environment from the perspective of how it feels to work there. What is the energy like when you walk the floors? If you have a lot of virtual or remote workers, how do you keep them connected to their teams? Make sure your work environment fuels your objectives and helps to get you to your goals.

7. **Do your employees feel appreciated and rewarded?** Create a culture that regularly rewards employees and creates a culture of appreciation. Look across the generations and see how Generation Y and the Baby Boomers have different expectations. Breeze back to chapter five and get some ideas about small rewards that go a long way.

8. **Where do you get your inspiration?** Think about what inspires you. Is it case studies like the ones in chapter six or taking care of your health? Or maybe creating a wellness program to make your entire organization healthier? Or even taking the lead from IBM and creating a service corps that recognizes top performers with volunteer sabbaticals.

9. **What is the one most important thing you need to accomplish as a leader right now?** Are you a poor listener? Do your younger team members see you as a technophobe or someone who is out of touch? Review the traits of outstanding leaders in chapter seven and think about what is holding you back the most and what can propel you forward.

10. **Where do you see yourself in 10, 20 or 30 years?** Think about how you want to define yourself as a leader and what the future of leadership is for you. Will you put your personal issues and ego aside for the benefit of the organization and its people? Will you build loyalty with your leadership and trust with your heart?

Magnetic Leadership, at its core, is about believing in and understanding people. What makes them tick. What they truly want. What they need to hear. How they want to believe. For many leaders, the most surprising thing is that it is often the simplest things that mean the most.

If I were to summarize the R.E.A.L. approach to Magnetic Leadership
in one sentence, I would say:

Bring your heart to work, and your employees will bring their heads.

Enjoy the R.E.A.L. journey of The Power of Magnetic Leadership!

Please Share Your Experience

I hope you learned something valuable in reading

The Power of Magnetic Leadership

or perhaps the insights presented helped you with a particular situation your business is facing.

Please take a moment and share your story and success with us.

Fax your response to (603) 334-3404
or
E-mail it to dmdurkin@loyaltyfactor.com.
Thank you, and we look forward to hearing from you.

_____

_____

_____

_____

_____

_____

Other books by Dianne M. Durkin

The Loyalty Factor
Building Employee, Customer and Brand Loyalty

Blueprint For Success
with Ken Blanchard and Stephen R. Covey

Purchase them at http://www.loyaltyfactor.com and also available on Amazon.

References

[i]   http://www.gallup.com/consulting/52/employee-engagement.aspx

[ii]   http://www.nikebiz.com/company_overview/

[iii]   http://www.starbucks.com/about-us/company-information/mission-statement

[iv]   http://www.thecoca-colacompany.com/ourcompany/mission_vision_values.html

[v]   JetBlue. 2005. Annual Report.

[vi]   http://www.wholefoodsmarket.com/company/corevalues.php

[vii]   Ayers, Keith E. 2008. Engagement is Not Enough: You Need Passionate Employees to Achieve your Dreams. Elevate.

[viii] Ayers, Keith E. 2008. Engagement is Not Enough: You Need Passionate Employees to Achieve your Dreams. Elevate.

[ix]   George, Bill with Peter Sims. 2007. True North: Discover your authentic Leadership. ll George with Peter Sims. San Francisco, CA: Jossey-Bass, a Wiley Imprint.

[x]   Dubrin, Andrew J. 2007. Leadership Research Findings, Practice, and Skills. Fifth Edition. Boston: Houghton Mifflin Company, 2007.

[xi]   Pfeiffer, J.W. and J.E. Jones, eds. 2007 (Revised). A Handbook of Structural Experiences for Human Relations Training, Vol. 1. San Diego, CA: University Associates Press.

[xii]   Dubrin, Andrew J. 2007. Leadership Research Findings, Practice, and Skills. Fifth Edition. Boston: Houghton Mifflin Company, 2007.

[xiii] Goleman, Daniel. 1995. Emotional Intelligence. New York, NY: Bantam Dell, A Division of Random House, Inc.

[xiv]   Dubrin, Andrew J. 2007. Leadership Research Findings, Practice, and Skills. Fifth Edition. Boston: Houghton Mifflin Company, 2007.

[xv]   Dubrin, Andrew J. 2007. Leadership Research Findings, Practice, and Skills. Fifth Edition. Boston: Houghton Mifflin Company, 2007.

xvi   Libove, Laurie Ribble. 1996. Learning to Listen. King of Prussia, PA: HRDQ.

xvii   http://www.entrepreneur.com/humanresources/managingemployees/article206318.html

xviii   2010 Fortune 100 Best Companies to Work For

xix   HR Magazine. September 2010. The Power of Incentive.

xx   Lancaster, Lynne C. and David Stillman. When Generations Collide at Work Quiz. http://humanresources.about.com/.

xxi   USA Today. Nov. 6, 2005. Generation Y: They've arrived at work with a new attitude. http://www.usatoday.com/money/workplace/2005-11-06-gen-y_x.htm

xxii   Schwartz, Tony. June 2010. The Productivity Paradox: How Sony Pictures Gets More Out of People by Demanding Less. Harvard Business Review.

xxiii   http://www.theenergyproject.com

xxiv   McLaughlin, Peter. September 2006. Fit to Be CEO: How some CEOs link fitness and Performance. The Chief Executive: http://findarticles.com/p/articles/mi_m4070/is_220/ai_n16808828/

xxv   Theorell, Tores, M.D., Ph.D. (Stockholm University) and Emil F. Coccaro, M.D (University of Chicago). June 24, 2010. Mad at Work? Don't have a Heart Attack. June 24, 2010. http://www.bottomlinesecrets.com/article.html?article_id=100001460

xxvi   http://blogs.hbr.org/imagining-the-future-of-leadership/2010/06/time-to-shift-the-paradigm-of.html

xxvii   http://blogs.hbr.org/imagining-the-future-of-leadership/2010/06/from-corporate-university-to-c-1.html

xxviii   http://blogs.hbr.org/imagining-the-future-of-leadership/2010/05/bringing-the-global-mindset-to.html

xxix   http://www.thunderbird.edu/sites/globe/

About the Authors

Dianne Durkin

Dianne Durkin is the president and founder of Loyalty Factor, a consulting and training company that enhances employee, customer and brand loyalty for some of the nation's most prominent corporations and smaller businesses. She has more than 25 years of experience in training and development, finance, direct sales and international marketing, and is widely recognized as a visionary thinker who has a rare combination of creativity and a strong business sense. Quick to assess the core issues within a company and outline their impact on the organization and its profits, productivity and people, she is continually requested to lead companies into new markets and in new directions, handle organizational restructures and set up programs to build lasting commitments with employees and customers.

Interviewed as the Loyalty Expert by ABC News, Dianne was featured in the New York Times, Wall Street Journal, Fortune, USA Today, Investor's Business Daily and the Boston Globe, among numerous other publications. She was the subject of two cover stories in Learning and Training magazine and Sales & Service Excellence.

A Stevie Award Finalist in two categories, "Women Helping Women" and "Website of the Year," Dianne is active in the Boston Club, Commonwealth Institute, CEO Club, Who's Who in America and Women in World Trade. She shares her knowledge and expertise in leadership as an adjunct professor at Plymouth State University and UMASS Lowell.

Carey Earle

Carey Earle collaborated with Dianne Durkin on this energizing book.

A serial entrepreneur and marketer who began her career on Madison Avenue, Carey has worked with some of the world's most respected brands and high-growth companies crafting adaptive marketing and brand strategies. A dynamic speaker, she has appeared on CNNfn, CNBC, Bloomberg and PBS, was featured in a documentary about women business owners called "Alpha Female," and also was quoted in: The New York Times, Fortune Small Business, Business Week, Working Woman, Adweek and American Demographics.

Carey is an adjunct instructor of marketing at New York University. She also lectures at her alma mater, American University, where she serves as a member of the Dean's Advisory Council for the School of Communication.